REBEL
ROMANCE

"For Dad"

REBEL
ROMANCE
Seductive Truth

PATCH SPEARS

XULON PRESS

Xulon Press
2301 Lucien Way #415
Maitland, FL 32751
407.339.4217
www.xulonpress.com

Paperback ISBN-13: 978-1-6628-2328-2
Hard Cover ISBN-13: 978-1-6628-2330-5
Ebook ISBN-13: 978-1-6628-2331-2

"Surely no rebel can expect the King to pardon his treason while he remains in open revolt."
~Charles Spurgeon

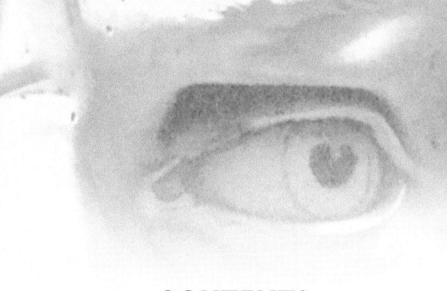

CONTENTS

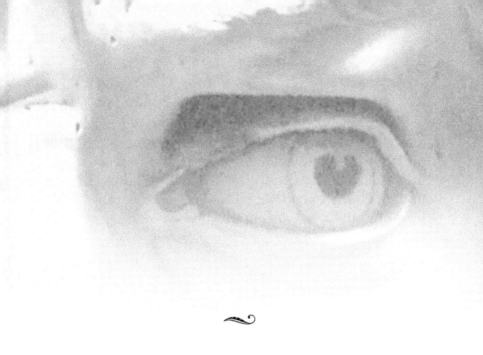

I could, quite literally, fill a book in dedication to those who have contributed to this vision. They are both enemy and friend alike. They are the gracefully angelic and the insidiously demonic who have engaged me throughout my journey. But every story has its preeminent Hero—its' triumphant King.

The boundary of human language does not permit the recognition due this King. I am forced, as well as inclined, to rely entirely on the all-sufficient power of His Name, and the fulfillment of His precious promises, to bring the ultimate tribute—*Jesus*, my Lord, and my God. All honor and glory are Yours. May Your love conquer, by whatever means necessary, every rebel heart.

To Andrea: Thank you for making me look like I know what I'm doing. Your exceptional skills have awakened in me a deep appreciation for what you do—not to mention the embarrassment you save those like me. Your gracious generosity is a blessing—a rare thing indeed.

Finally, to my best friend who, by God's infinite wisdom, is also my wife. Tricia, your sacrificial and peacefully supportive way is priceless. I have never met another human with such seemingly natural grace, patience, and tact. Such tact is easily overlooked, but the impact of your unique ability to cultivate peace is immeasurable. I am forever grateful for you and the love we share.

"No doubt pain, as God's megaphone, is a terrible instrument. It may lead to final and unrepented rebellion. But it gives the only opportunity the bad man can have for amendment. It removes the veil; it plants the flag of truth within the fortress of a rebel soul."
C.S. Lewis~ "The Problem of Pain"

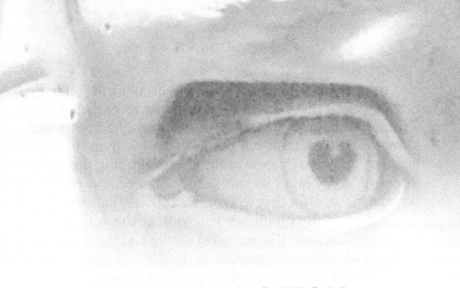

INTRODUCTION

To write about the mystery of God is, and should be, a daunting thing. The responsibility of such an endeavor keeps many from it. One can only reflect and echo the words and ways of God. No man or woman can speak directly for God, aside from the power of the Holy Spirit, and has no authority but that which is given him by the great commission our Lord has commanded and called us to.

That said, no person can spend consistent time in the presence of God, drinking in His words, walking in His "wake," contemplating His wisdom, or basking in the light of His love, and keep silent about it.

To say anything about the character of God brings onto us an indescribable, dueling dynamic of reverence for the truth in balance with the inescapable passion to make Him known. To fall in love with Jesus is to talk about Him—at times like that insufferable friend who has just met the girl of his dreams.

I have been writing for the better part of my life and it is no accident that I have only somewhat recently begun writing publicly about God. It is not that I had nothing to say of Him till now, but the fact that I will meet Him one day, and give an answer for it, is a sobering thought foremost in my mind. James said, "Let not many of you become teachers for they will receive a stricter judgement."

In this small volume we will look at the ways God "romances" us, as well as our rebel nature and the ongoing struggle with that nature, even in the life and writings of this author.

As significant the burden of conveying the truth, and as much as is at stake to *get it right,* as Jeremiah lamented, I cannot be quiet!

I know my Lord's heart has one all-pervading purpose—to save those who are separated from Him—to fill them with that which their soul craves—with the only treasure that satisfies the needs of humanity. How could anyone have the cure for a deadly disease (let alone death itself) and keep it to themselves? To know the truth of this life and hide it would indeed be as dark and insidious an action as any other.

Before you walk through this book with me, I want you to know, *it is important to know,* who you are reading. Deception begins by looking at the wrong thing in the first place.

Where is the writer coming from? There are those who will write anything—who are bound by few principles, self-driven, and accountable to no one. To write about truth, you must spend time with truth. One must be able to instantly recognize what *is not* truth. One must study long and hard the genuine bank note, in order to develop the ability to spot the counterfeit.

Without this "curing," one has no business writing about truth or teaching others. This is in no way to imply that I am special. I believe that anyone who will commit, with sincere diligence, to sitting at the feet of Jesus, in worship and prayer, saturated with the Word of God, over time, cannot come away without this ability. The Holy Spirit of God is, as Jesus called Him, "The Spirit of Truth." He cannot abide falsity, deception, or any form of evil, and in His presence, error is exposed.

My prayer for you is that, like the Berean Jews, you will "receive the message with great eagerness and examine the scriptures daily (for yourself) to see if what is told you is true." (Acts 17:11) It is far too important to simply take anyone else's word for it—including mine.

"Draw near to God and He will draw near to you."
(James 4:8)

"Call to me and I will answer you and show you great and mighty things you do not know."
(Jeremiah 33:3)

I can offer here the philosophical perspectives I have gleaned in the presence of God, but my primary motive, the mission of my heart, is to introduce you to *Him*, and urge you to go to *Him*—to call on *Him*—to sit with *Him*— to allow *Him* to pull back the curtain on the greatest mystery of life. The words of men concerning Jesus have far surpassed that of any other subject in history, but none of them will suffice to convince you. They are but signposts directing humanity down a path, leading to a door. To stop short of opening that door will say nothing of the map which led you there.

Much greater writers have been ridiculed for the maps they have drawn. The failing incompetence of a map maker will never negate the fact that a place exists. And regardless how many arguments are made or how many mock the reality of the existence of a place, one thing is certain—that place is either there, or it is not. No opinion can either remove it or validate it.

That is the undeniable solidity of Truth—it stands completely unaffected by belief. It is the one thing which depends on nothing other than itself and will not be altered. Whatever may come against it can never overcome its power. Truth will outlast all attempts to destroy it. One of the names given to Jesus, Who said, "I AM the Truth," is "The Rock," and like a massive granite rock on the seashore of eternity, no amount of time, no constant barrage of the waves of offense or denial will move or degrade it.

"Heaven and earth will pass away, but My Words
will never pass away." (Matthew 24:35)

I can think of nothing more pitiful, or unnecessarily regretful, than those souls who have been offered the map of truth and tossed it aside, or even worse, those who reached the end of the path and refused to open the door and enter in.

My prayer is that you will not be one of these. I would be lying to say that my *chief* concern ventured much further than my own family. Maybe you can relate. Of course, to see the world through God's eyes and with His heart sparks compassion for *all* who are without Christ, but my heart breaks to think, to *know*, that some who are closest and most dear to me may live with a dangerous confidence in respect to the notion of eternal loss.

Many feel that a God who would make it so difficult to believe in Him is ridiculous. But I would suggest that they ask themselves, if that is indeed the case, why their thoughts of Him are so frequent? Maybe it is because almost every aspect of society presents Him. Maybe it is because, at almost every turn in our lives, we are inundated or reminded by something which reflects Him in some manner. Or maybe the whisper of Truth is their constant companion.

How is it that a poor Carpenter who lived over 2000 years ago, in a remote village, somehow split our history into the time before He came and the time after? Ever consider this?

Why is this Man, Who never went to college, never wrote a book, never held an office, never traveled more than 200 miles from the place He was born, had no house of His own, spent only 3 years in ministry, and was killed by the age of 33, *the most* celebrated, loved, and followed figure the world has ever known? Why is the instrument of His demise the most recognized and revered symbol in the history of mankind? It would take much more faith than I have to believe these things a mere coincidence.

In the end, we all have the free will to deny another's love, even the love of God; and, in the end, we all have our own free will to deny what we are told- even when it is Truth itself.

In the end we are all left with only one real choice when it comes to God- union with Him, or rebellion against Him.

And in the end, no other choice you will ever make will matter more.

What if there were something keeping us, obstructing us, from a view of true reality? What if what is true for the body, that it suffers disease, is just as true for the spirit? What if humans were exposed to, and infected with, a spiritual virus that was passed on from parent to child, without exception, from the very beginning of our existence? What if that spiritual infection so blinded us to what we were before it that we reject the very thought of it as absurd?

"What happened to you, Patch?"

I believe my purpose to be about little more than answering that very question—to give reasons, with every ability God has given me, for the hope that is within me.

The answer to this question, to some, may seem peculiar, fanciful, or even ludicrous. But my life, like our history timeline, was divided into the days and years before Christ, and those which came after Him. Growing up, I was taught about Jesus and I did believe in Him, but mostly because I *wanted* Him to be real. Then, one day He arrived, in my very presence, and lifted the veil to reveal a reality I could not unsee. The spiritual virus was healed, eradicated, removed from me, and I was no longer blind to what we as humans were before the fall.

Suddenly, like awakening from a dream, I found that all I had thought to be true had been an illusory presentation of an incomplete picture. Instead of observing the frayed and tangled knots, and indiscriminately crossing threads, the embroidered tapestry had been flipped over to reveal a beautifully crafted masterpiece. So many seemingly random inconsistencies fell, or rather, were drawn together into order. I stood in amazement as I was shown how all the jagged pieces fit!

I turned to look through the scattered, clumsy, and staggering idiocies of my life to see they had been brilliantly orchestrated into a symphony of unlikely purpose. There was no reasonable explanation for this but that Someone, with infinite means, had been intimately involved and intently engaged with me at every bungled turn and in every tiny detail of my existence.

All I had thought to be horrid happenstance, curious coincidence, or stupendous blunder, had been made strangely indispensable to a perfectly managed itinerary. No inventory was left uncounted, nothing discarded as insignificant, not a single shaving of a moment's material wasted—not one tear left to dry—not one pain or throbbing heartache unused. Purpose engulfed me. Peace sustained me. Joy and amazement compelled me, knowing, *truly* knowing, that He was in control—That He had always, and would always, be directing my path.

He had embraced the thorns that had pricked and bled us both, placed them into our garden, and cultivated them into bright and thriving roses. He had taken my rebellion and used it to romance me.

So, *this* is the writer you have considered reading. Not the theologian, though God has taught me. Not the pastor, though He has called me to preach. Not the novice, though there is much still to learn. Not the fanatic, though I think of little else—but the ragged rebel soul who has been pursued and captured by the relentless love of God— one who has met Him, knows Him, and is compelled by the grace of purpose to make Him known.

There are two kinds of people. There are rebels, and then, there are rebels. The truth is, whatever your beliefs, you are a rebel of some kind. We are all resisting something. The question is: Which rebellion most reasonably deserves our honor? Which cause is at once most noble and most anemic?

Not everyone wants to be on the right side. In fact, some are vehemently opposed to anything that even smells of righteousness. They literally cannot bear the very notion of it.

Some will pose behind a pride in a rebellion pathetically harbored as a mysteriously "cool," dark, romance with lawlessness. Others rise against submission as a false threat to grace, forgetting love is qualified by obedience, and belief and compliance are allies. Others still are slaves to a law they cannot keep—in love with their correction of those who share that limitation—convinced they can cross the chasm on their own backs.

But for the grownups in the room—for those who understand the timeless authenticity of true wisdom—that shallow existence won't do. For the humble few, a genuine rebel romance—the established Ever, the ancient and poetic True, is not created, but discovered—not crafted, portrayed, or even drawn out, but rather entered into.

It is that which is found once all pretense, pride, and presumption fall away. It is what has always been. It is the mountain revealed, still standing, when the clouds of duplicity give way to the winds of humility, and one sees the Mind that holds the truth of life is not his own, and never could be. When one comes to the lucid revelation his greatest threat is no more than his very own passions, then, concedes all he has so desperately embraced as romance is his preeminent foe, the veritable dissent, the legit rebellion of the ages, can finally begin.

One will never leave a salient mark on the world, his city, his family, or eternity till he has rallied the resistance within, and found himself wanting—till he has first allowed the Flag of victory to be planted in the once rancid valley of his own soul.

The greatest, most significant act of rebellion is inexplicably counterintuitive. It is surrender—complete and utter surrender to the cause which opposes almost everything about us.

~Patch

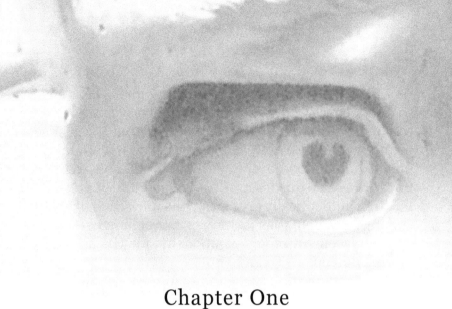

Chapter One

ROMANCING REBELS

"Today I begin to understand what love must be, if it exists... when we are parted, we each feel the lack of the other half of ourselves. We are incomplete like a book in two volumes of which the first has been lost. That is what I imagine love to be; incompleteness in absence."
~Edmond de Goncourt

So often I ponder what great benefit it could be to those souls who walk through this world without the manifest power, presence, and provision of God, if somehow, they were to step into this reality for a day. What a difference that day would make. To see all that the child of God passes over when in conversation with them, unable to put into words the innumerable favors displayed by the love of God. Today was just such a day.

This manifold and mysterious wisdom of God is such that any effective attempt to recount or accurately portray its complex manifestations with significant justice cannot be found. Soren Kierkegaard said that "Life can only be understood backwards, but it must be lived forward." It is also this frustrating dynamic which prevents me from authentically presenting the intricacies of God's comings and goings as it were, or more directly His sovereign placement of key components for His apparent desired outcome— To love you.

Lest you question the stability in my logic, then consider Kierkegaard's point: "If, in all our collective sagacity, we conclude that we cannot believe in the things which cannot be seen with our eyes then, first and foremost, we must no longer continue to believe in love."

To collect the day's events and set out to piece together the puzzle of divine provision, solely in the last twenty-four hours, and place them on the page so that they were understood for the true purposes they carry, and the attentive love which was expressed concerning their manner of carefully appointed happenstance, would pathetically diminish the splendor of a masterpiece. I can but use one word or else make a mess of it... *Romance.*

I know, I know. I'm a writer. Conveying the true picture, plot, passion, and purpose, is what I do!

Look, I can describe for you the multifaceted prism of competing emotions that flood the body and mind the first time you jump out of an airplane from fourteen-thousand feet. I can tell you the initial fear that your chute might not open fades in the beauty and adrenaline of an eagles view even before it does. And I can attempt to translate the slightly contested disappointment when your chute *does* open and the freedom of the 120 mile-an-hour freefall, an experience you will *never* have again, is abruptly over. Now, I can't speak for everyone, but I can tell you that soaring under your canopy above everything, in the most exciting silence you'll ever know, cannot last long enough and all you can think about, even before you've landed, is how soon you can do it again.

I can tell you that you will never look at the sky in quite the same way. I can say with Leonardo da Vinci, "For once you have tasted flight you will forever walk the earth with your eyes turned skyward, for there you have been and there you will long to return."

I can tell you all these things and perhaps you can imagine with me to some extent what that experience could be like. But I tell you that I could write a hundred books in the effort to bring you into those moments and never scratch the surface of its true reality. It is the same when trying to project an authentic impartation of the peculiar reality in relationship with the presence of God. The true representation can only be realized when delivered by the very hand of God Himself.

Having stated this, you might think, *"Well, what's the point then? You can end the book right here!"* From the time I was a little boy, I have wanted to fly—to soar above the earth like a bird. I used to have dreams in which I did just that. In my dream, I would run as fast as I could down an old farm road and if I could get going fast enough, I would begin to lift right off the ground until I was gliding over the top of a big red barn and the stables and past a towering wheat bin. I think it was all born from watching the magical car flown by Dick Van Dyke, in the movie "Chitty Chitty Bang Bang".

In my simple little world at eight-years-old it was nothing more than a dream, and as I carried it through the years it seemed all the less likely to ever come true. Until I was about thirty and came home from work one day to a message on my answering machine.

For anyone born after 1990 we had these tape recorder machines that hooked up to what we called a "land line" because back then it was the only way you knew if you missed a call. Anyway, as the message played, I heard one of my buddies saying they were going skydiving that day and I better hurry if I wanted to ride down to Granbury with them and "jump out of a perfectly good airplane."

All the sudden, my dream was possible! If I really wanted it, there were experienced skydivers who would show me how I, myself, could actually fly like a bird! And if I were strong enough to push back the fear, listen to what they said, and take a leap of faith, I could experience what they had. I would not just *hear* about how it felt or *watch* someone else do it. If I made that choice, I would be living it, for real, that very day.

What if I had missed that call or decided not to believe my buddy and thought it was all a hoax- make believe- too good to be true? What if I'd just considered the risk too great and found an excuse not to go? *"Maybe I'll just tell him I'll go next time. This sounds a little extreme. What if I become a skydiving fanatic and it upsets my life? What if people think I'm crazy or even weird?"* Yeah, let me tell you this; I would have missed out on the greatest experience of my life at the time.

What I would like to do is take you somewhere for a little while and show you how to fly. Would that be ok? I promise it won't hurt. In fact, you too could come along with us and taste flight and forever walk the earth with your eyes and heart turned skyward, for there you will have been and there you will always long to return.

I'd like to take you with me on a brief hike through the mountains of truth and then right to the edge of a deep crevasse where few dare to visit. I want us to pause at the cliff's brim and allow the eyes of our hearts to scan an often hidden but very real and wonderful valley in the kingdom and character of God.

I hope as we explore these fringes and carefully descend the solid rock facing of the power and majesty of our Lord, you will discover the fragrant and quietly subdued bliss of this velvet-lined meadow. Butterflies dance to the music of white doves, over crystal-clear waters cascading a path down the valley wall into a peaceful lagoon. A few crisp sunbeams break a canopy of clouds to highlight a runaway grove of cherry blossoms and their miniature white petals strewn across the mirrored pond's reflection of the rising mountain peaks.

We have no problem recognizing the power and strength in the mountainous muscle of God. But do we allow this to obstruct an expedition in search of the tranquil, intimate valleys winding deep into the heart of God? Are we so captured by His Royalty that we miss His romance?

God has invited us time and again to seek Him as silver, search for Him as buried treasure, draw near to Him, and call to Him.

What I want us to see is all the ways He seeks us, pursues us, draws us, gropes, or reaches for us, "returns" to us, chases, and overtakes us! From the moment He created His beloved mankind, His desire has been to love us—for Him to be ours and for us to be His. Our almighty God, our Creator is our greatest Friend who has relentlessly courted us. He is our Bridegroom, and we are His bride.

When the word seduction first came to mind, I thought it somewhat inappropriate because, in the vernacular of our current day, seduction is typically connected to sexual innuendo. However, the Latin root of the word "seducere" means to "draw aside" or "to draw to one's self."

When a man is attracted to a woman he will, at some point, draw her aside to get to know her better. We all know that often it is easier to meet someone for the first time in a group setting but when there is an obvious connection, or desire for an individual, it is necessary to test the mutual meter and your initial feelings by having a one on one, say over coffee, or dinner, or perhaps a picnic at the park. This is "drawing aside." *This*, by its very definition, is seduction.

The Lord of all creation has been working to "draw us aside" or "seduce" us since the very beginning. The bible says we are the apple of His eye—the object of His affection—the loving relationship He has always desired. In fact, He has "loved us with an everlasting love and *drawn* us with unfailing kindness." (Jeremiah 31:3)

Romance is defined as a feeling of excitement and mystery associated with love (passion, adoration, devotion, affection, fondness). Paul speaks of "the *mystery* that has been kept hidden for ages... but now is revealed to the Lord's people." *Romantic* is defined as conducive to, or characterized by, the expression of love. I would suggest that the greatest expression of love in all of history was performed at a Roman cross 2000 years ago. (Colossians 1:26)

Is God a Romantic? Is our Lord really seducing us, courting us, romancing us?

When we go back to our beginning, our genesis, a picture of our Creator is revealed as a loving Father creating us in His image. We find He has created a wondrous and magical paradise and placed us in it to live an amazing existence. He walked and talked with us every day in an intimately personal relationship of provision, protection, and preeminence over the world He had given us. Nothing separated us from Him and there was constant active expression of His great love for us.

Social customs and tolerances have changed somewhat in the modern world, and even radically in the last two decades, but throughout the history of mankind men have typically been the initiator and pursuers in romantic things.

Not long ago, an honorable man would first come to the father of the young woman to which he found himself attracted and ask for permission, or the father's blessing, to "court" (respectfully pursue) his daughter for the purpose of presenting himself to both her and her family as a "suitor," or candidate, for her hand in marriage. This coordinated and principled custom might start when a young lady was about fifteen and could last into her twenties, depending on her options or impatient affections. Suffice it to say, this "courtship" could go on for many years.

This honored social custom has been passed down in fewer and fewer families to this day in mostly conservative regions or independent circles of society.

To understand the bedrock principles of marriage you must understand the character of God for He is the Creator of marriage. God instituted the very first marriage with the very first man and woman.

It was His idea, His creation, and God creates nothing without purpose. He created it as one of His most revealing gifts to be entered into by a man and woman, for the woman was perfectly created for man. Marriage joined the man and woman as sanctified (set apart) to each other, aside from all others in their union.

The Bible says they become one flesh, one made from two. This picture is presented to reveal the relationship God desires with us.

As Adam was naming the animals, the Bible states that no comparable partner was found for him. This implies he was looking for and desiring one. It was in his nature to desire this companion, this relationship, for one reason. He was made in the image of God, and we are shown a facet of God's character by understanding this truth.

Jesus prayed that we would be one with Him, as He is One with the Father, and that we become one together with them in the Spirit of God. (John 17:21) This is marriage, becoming *one*. God has made it clear, that we the church (the body of Christ), are the bride of Christ. He is our Bridegroom.

I think it obvious that it is plainly pictured in this way, as being His bride and also His body, that we are one with Him by faith. Now, I may rock a boat or two, as the truth often does, but I must address the notion that God would accept "Adam and Steve" as an authentic marriage.

Twenty years ago I would have been obliged to leave this subject to personal council and off the pages of this book. It has been my observation that this subject interjects itself as common confrontation on almost any occasion which speaks of matrimony. So, for the sake of our children and those raising them in this current day and the fact that in every schoolyard, contestant show, news cycle and indeed every medium of man, this generations "progressive" agenda seeks to present "alternate" lifestyles as flippantly casual and dangerously inconsequential as their chosen hairstyle— a voice of reason must be presented.

We are all adults here, so let's put away the giggles and smirks for a minute and just look at things logically. Setting aside the spiritual for a moment, let us simply use common sense and practical reason. Let's try an experiment. But first, let me preface the following anecdotes by stating that homosexuality is no different than fornication, adultery, or any other sin in the sense that it is any worse. Sin is sin.

We are simply attempting to reason the obvious order of our natural world and our collective experience to expose a truth, within the character of a God of order, for certain purposes within that creation, and what those ordered purposes are and are not. Again, this experiment is a practical and independent view of facts and common-sense circumstances for the benefit of establishing physical order and purpose; not withstanding emotional challenges inherent in human desire or temptation.

I'd like you to take the USB cable and unplug it from your laptop. Now, reverse the ends so that the end plugged into the wall socket can be inserted into your laptop (if you have no laptop, you may try the same with a phone charger). Now, plug the wall socket end into your laptop... I'll wait. Ok, scratch that. Go outside and repeat the process with your garden hose. Take the end connected to the house faucet (spigot) off, reverse the ends and attach the opposite end to the spigot... again, I'll wait. Ok, so then grab a pencil and tighten down the screws in your door hinges. Next, start your car with a fork, chop up your wood with a broom, sweep your floor with an axe, brush your teeth with a hairbrush or your hair with a toothbrush.

These exercises don't work for one reason. These objects are being asked to perform or fit a purpose for which they were not created. If a created thing fails to perform a purpose, it is, by all logical reasoning, useless and contrary to the function you are forcing on it and was obviously never designed for that purpose. Even if you are able to awkwardly improvise some level of success, you must, in honest logic, ask yourself "Is *this* purposed for *that*?"

One can pound in a nail with a shoe, (I know, I've done it) but with the choice of a hammer, you must ask "Is the shoe *right* or *wrong* for this purpose?"

Certain things are made for a predetermined purpose and logically we find folly in, and laugh at, the notion of interchanging the objects of our creation for something other than their intended purpose. Who brushes their teeth with a hairbrush?

In the first chapter of Romans this principle is plainly addressed. "They exchanged the truth about God for a lie... because of this; God gave them over to shameful lusts. Even their women exchanged *natural* sexual relations for *unnatural* ones. In the same way the men also abandoned *natural relations with women* and were inflamed with lust for *one another.* Men committed *shameful acts with other men* and received in themselves the due penalty for their error. Furthermore, just as they did not think it worthwhile to retain the knowledge of God, so God gave them over to a *depraved mind,* so that they do what *ought not to be done.*" (Romans 1:25-28) I didn't say it, God did. So, if you have a problem with it, take it up with Him.

Men and women fit each other perfectly in a physical sense but also psychologically and emotionally. Now, I know what you're thinking, "Whatever! That's just not always true!" But it is. There is a balance in the dynamic of the male-female relation and God in His often-misread wisdom has purposed this balance carefully. I'll refer you to a book by Dr. Emerson Eggerichs titled "*Love and Respect,*" which sheds great insight on this perfect balance. All God has created, said, or done is on purpose and for purpose.

In recent years, the gay community has experienced an explosion of "freedom" and an adamant proclamation of their "rightful" place in society as well as their constitutional civil rights of any entitlement owed or presently provided any other minority group.

I am not here to argue against their civil liberties under the law of the land except when their liberties seek to infringe on someone else's. By the laws of our nation's democracy, their way of life may be acceptable and even proper and instituted in the eyes of the law of man. However, they are clearly and without question unnatural, in opposition to, and unacceptable in the eyes of the law of God.

Like all sin, whether adultery, fornication, incest, pedophilia, pornography or any other sexual sin, homosexuality is a perversion of the naturally intended purpose of sex which is a gift within the sanctity of marriage to be shared by the man and woman as one for pleasure and the procreation of the human race. The order and purpose are obvious to anyone who has ever had sex or witnessed the miracle of childbirth. The pieces fit perfectly (naturally) and the purpose evident.

If we take a puzzle piece from one box and attempt to make it fit into a puzzle from another box, with a different purposed picture, it will never work. Evil seeks to take what God has made perfect and create a skewed copy of it. Satan is the romantic opponent of God. That bad boy, who proclaims his love and commitment, but in truth, is only out to use you for his selfish pleasure until he has taken your innocence, ruined your name and casts you underfoot like a splintered toothpick.

If we will just shut off the noise and think honestly about the people, things or ideas being offered us, it's really not that hard to spot the counterfeit.

Again, our discussion is not about desire. There are people who have all kinds of desires which we do not consider natural (incest, rape, murder, pedophilia). In fact, we consider these desires unnatural and unacceptable. We are simply looking at what may be reasoned as *natural* (intended by nature). "If homosexuality is *truly natural*, then why did nature give homosexual men bodies designed for reproductive sex with women and then give them desires for sex with men? Why would nature give desires for one type of sex but a body for another?" ~Gregory Koukl, *"Tactics"*

My pastor taught a series called "Tough Questions" and made an incredibly revealing point of application for those who believe and say they were "born this way." Also setting spiritual perspective aside, he took us through the logic of the evolutionist and secular mindset to show not just the improbability of, but the scientific impossibility that a "gay gene" could exist. After all, this is precisely what people are claiming by stating they are born gay. That it is innate, in their DNA makeup, and therefore it would be absurd that God would hold them accountable for something they had no control over. Their claim is that homosexuality is *natural.*

If this "gay gene" had ever evolved, it would have obviously had to begin with one person, the very first to have had the gene. Let's go there for a moment and hypothetically suppose this mutation took place. In order for that gene (in the first person to have it) to be passed on to later generations, the original carrier of that gene would have had to have children. Because he (let's say it was a man) was only attracted to his own sex, he would not produce an offspring. The same is true with women.

The only way to procreate is through male/female intercourse. Therefore, that supposed "gay gene" would not have survived past the first generation. This is simply because it was not natural and not designed and purposed to do so. If everyone were to wake up gay tomorrow, the earth's population, and subsequently the human race, would cease to exist by the beginning of the next century!

The question is not, "Can it work *physically?*" or "Why not?" The real question is, "Does it make sense *naturally?*" If it does, then why not create one sex in the first place? Why are all living things created male and female? And if we decide that one unnatural behavior is *acceptable* then what's to stop our rationalization that all may be so?

"I can't help it!" they say. Now, to say those living this lifestyle are born with it in the sense that they are born sinful in nature, with a tainted propensity to desire to pursue sin, is valid. But that's all of us!

So, do we say, "I was born an adulterer, so I can't help cheating on my wife?" "I was born a liar, so, my boss can't fire me for lying. That's discrimination!" If someone claims, "I can't help it, I was born incestuous, or a pedophile!" Do we then just allow his behavior with no discriminatory action? "I was born a thief... a murderer..."

Does it somehow make these sins okay if we just believe we can live out any idea no matter its consequence, or how unnatural it may be, because we simply say we are born that way? God loves everyone who's ever lived and wants each one to turn to Him. He doesn't hate the sinner. He hates the cancer of sin within us. At some point, you must ask yourself where this perversion of truth and purpose end. Where's the line? How much "tolerance" is too much? What are the parameters? Are there parameters? It takes very little research into our culture today to force us to consider this question.

It's being seriously suggested that everyone should be able to self-identify as whatever they want, whether it's gender, ethnicity, age, or even what planet they're from. Who are we to say what or who they are? We shouldn't offend!

Today parents are insisting that no specific gender be given to their newborn infant. They have left that box unchecked as to male or female and instead have declared that they will allow their child to self-identify as whatever they choose. Yea! If you've been living under a rock for the last five years and just now hearing this fact, welcome to the "Twilight Zone."

A month ago, I witnessed an interview with a "family" who told the true story of a 60-year-old man who decided he no longer self-identified as a 60-year-old man but an 8-year-old little girl. A family in California consisting of a 40 something year-old couple and their (actual) 9-year-old daughter had adopted this 60-year-old man and were being interviewed on a TV show as this very confused older man sat there between them all, wearing a blue dress, pigtails, and holding a teddy bear. He talked in a high and tiny tone as he thought an 8-year-old girl would. It was completely "legit."

I cannot imagine the long-term, irreparable damage this biological daughter of 9 would sustain while enduring the mind bending and socially retarding effect of this pathetic nonsense!

Again, the question: Where does this craziness stop? If a child self-identifies as an adult, will they be allowed to marry an adult? If a pedophile self-identifies as a child, must his presence and behavior be accepted? What if people start self-identifying as animals?!

If you think about it, I think you'll agree this "relative truth" ideology, this "tolerance," this anti-offense narrative, can take us to some very dark places and yield some disturbingly bizarre results. The more one thing is accepted, the easier it is for the next thing to follow. The absurd is unheard-of, a radical thought then proposed, and then justified next to the no longer unheard-of, and then strangely acceptable, and then acceptable, and then common place, and *then* praised, and then an afterthought—while the next absurdity moves up in line.

Listen. Before you add any more to the sketched picture you may be drawing of me, I have very good friends who are self-described as gay that I've known all my life. I think no less of them than I do any of God's beloved. I visit them, have dinner with them, laugh with them, and cry with them from time to time. I don't judge them by their challenges any more than I want to be judged by mine. They know what I believe, and they have known my challenges. They know I believe we must all be honest with ourselves and as a writer that honesty comes out on the page.

My responsibility is first to the truth of my Lord and my love for Him which then allows me to love them with the compassion He shows me. I was a very sick person battling the powerful monster known as alcohol and many were the casualties of that war.

Years ago, the brother of my best friend at the time was living a homosexual lifestyle and suffering from AIDS. I was recently separated from my wife and at a very low and dark place when I visited them in Seattle. Though not a Christian, this man had gained a completely new view of life in light of the possibilities he faced in his recently discovered affliction. He helped me see some things about life I had forgotten and just wasn't seeing at the time. I was in no position to help myself, let alone him. But he helped me, and I am forever grateful that he cared enough to do so.

The thing to remember is that we are all fighting our own battles. We are all living in a fallen world and trying to find our way. No matter who we are, we have this in common. No matter what our sin of choice, Jesus calls *all* to call on His name and be saved. There is a place of restoration and healing from that sin at the foot of the cross.

But one thing I learned is, the truth is the truth regardless of what we think of it or what challenges we have in accepting it. "Tolerance" for the sake of tolerance alone excludes the need for checks and balances and this, along with the idea of "relative truth," hinders us from calling out evil in the interest of universal inclusion. If doctors saw their patients the way some see the world, they would not seek to remove disease for fear of denying its "rightful" place in the nature of things.

As the common mindset of a society's moral compass is compromised to say that "sometimes south is north," eventually "sometimes" becomes "half the time," and then, eventually, south becomes the *new* north "all the time."

The wrong direction has been accepted for so long, it is actually seen as the right direction. Look at all we called evil just fifty years ago that is now being called good. Look at all we once called good that is now considered evil. This progression does not simply stop on its own.

The prophet Isaiah foretold of this time. "Woe to those who call evil good and good evil, who put darkness for light and light for darkness, who put bitter for sweet and sweet for bitter. Woe to those who are wise in their *own* eyes and clever in their *own* sight." (Isaiah 5:20-21)

When we decide to choose what's morally right and wrong based on individual human perspectives then truth becomes relative to each person. Our incessant need these days to prevent any appearance of offense to anyone overrides our responsibility to draw clear lines and erect solid borders of common sense, much less right and wrong.

As I wrote the previous line, I could see some of the younger writers today placing the phrase "right and wrong" in quotations, as I have just now, because they see it just that way, *relative*, open to interpretation. Right and wrong are anything but open to interpretation, for when they are, they quite easily trade places.

One of the most attractive manifestations in people is their honesty and commitment to be straight forward with you.

I think of the contrast between past relationships I have endured where this was not the case and the marriage I enjoy today where maturity reveals an understanding. It is essential that we be true to ourselves and to each other about our feelings, challenges, and circumstantial reality, setting aside the hindrance that is offense, when expecting the truth. Knowing that whether our convictions come out as affirming praise or constructively critical, they are born and intended in love.

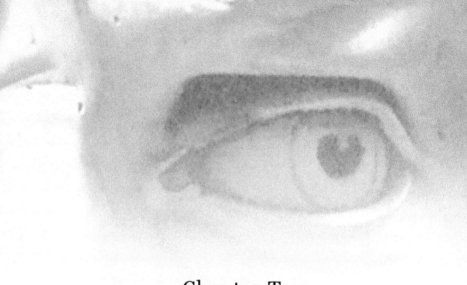

Chapter Two

GOOD NEWS!

~⌒

"All the beautiful sentiments in the world weigh less than a single lovely action."
~James Russell Lowell

I read a post on Facebook from a man's perspective which stated, "If I say something that can be taken two different ways, I meant it the good way."

People read the Ten Commandments and take the "Thou shalt nots" or the "You will nots" as from a God who just likes to step on their fun, when in fact, we lovingly say the same to our children.

"You will not play in the street."

"Thou shalt not hit your sister."

"Thou shalt not watch too much TV or play video games too long."

We don't create or enforce these rules to take away their fun but because we love them and want to protect them. The commandments of God are born and intended in love. If you did not place parameters, rules, and discipline in the lives of your children you would be hurting them, not loving them. God's rules are there *for* you, *not* to spite you. Why do we refuse to make this connection between *our* responsible and loving parental obligations and that of God's?

The less we see the prominence of God in our society, the more we see misbehavior, disorder, and flat-out chaos in the world. What happens when a teacher leaves a classroom of young students for an extended period? You remember Jr. High, don't you?

The room gradually gets restless. The volume ascends at about the same rate the seconds tick off. Soon, students are out of their chairs, across the room, playing music, throwing things, wrestling, and chasing each other around. If left unchecked too long, it is likely the classroom would erupt in flames! The teacher's return is felt with a shout as she stands at the doorway in appalling amazement.

This is a picture of our world without God and His rules of morality adjusting our tendency to cross the line. Not long ago, you could hear Him in the halls of humanity shouting "No! North is *still* north, south *still* south."

"Progressive" ideology and relative truth will, *if not checked*, see our society in increasing levels of chaos and confusion having no compass with which to adjust our direction. This compass is not purposed for control, in the way some think, but for protection and from compassion in a loving Father who does not want His children destroyed.

If we think our sin is any less egregious or damaging than someone else's then we are missing the big picture. We all have a cancerous disease which separates us from God and subsequently from a good life beyond this world.

Any sin, all sin, precludes us from entering the presence of our Holy God. Light is always a dispelling force to darkness. Darkness is precluded from existence in the presence of light.

This is precisely our predicament in relation to God. Until we see that, we will never understand the need we have of Jesus or the good that God *is* and has *always been* toward us.

From about the time I was nine years old, I was intrigued with rebellion. In later years, my mother was horrified to hear my brothers and I telling stories such that she never imagined her little boys would have ever been engaged. Some kids start out in a commonly known practice of knocking on doors and bolting to a hiding place to observe the aggravated grown-up. Others wasted their parent's toilet paper just to imagine someone's surprise when heading out to work the next day.

There is a long list of these types of adolescent trickeries, and I not only participated, but became a creative force to impress my peers with an evolution of original ways to occupy our summer nights. One thing drove me more than any other—amusing girls. I realized quite early that the bolder my actions were, the more attention they gave me. I suppose, at some point, all men learn this.

To girls, we are all basically the same until something is introduced that separates us from the pack. As you mature, you come to see that this something must express a devotion, a commitment, or a convincing statement of action, that dispels any doubt about our feelings for them. The most effective vehicle for this purpose is risk or sacrifice of some kind.

We could delve deep here into a complex theology permeating the gospel of Christ and the multi-faceted plan to solve the problem of a separation between man and his Creator, but the faith of the mind lays out the architectural blueprints, while our heart simply stands back in awe of the building's beauty. Let us set aside the genius of the redemption plan and simply look at the magnitude of the expressive nature of the cross.

I suggest that no alternative act could have equaled the sacrifice exhibited by the only Fathered Son of our Creator to extravagantly, and so completely, dispel any doubt as to our God's devotion and commitment to us. In the occasion of any dispute of God's character, this solitary truth should end all argument in an instant.

Whether or not he was aware, as mankind sat in utter darkness and despair, the God of all creation entered into his world of dire circumstance. Facing the power of death, indeed the prince of darkness, and the enemy of the souls of men, He decisively conquered forever our greatest foe in the most magnificent display of love, courage and chivalry the eternal universe would ever know. Men foolishly say they would believe if they could see. Well then, open your eyes and behold! It has never been hidden, in fact, it was sufficiently foretold.

Men see what they want to see, and such is the mind of man that he be so foolish as to think that if he closes his eyes to uncomfortable things, they would go away or never have been so. This is the five-year-old child in us. My mother tells of my attempts at this as a little boy. I would stand against a wall, close my eyes, and turn my head, and believe that because I could see nothing, no one could see me.

Listen, again, until we see the problem, we will not see how beautiful the solution, what it cost, and what it means for us in relation to God. Accordingly, we will not come to know the depth of the love within the character of God until we discern the weight of what is at stake without His active love.

Follow me. If you do not know Christ as Savior, there is a sinister *being* with court authority coming, warrant in hand, for your arrest. It is a legal warrant obtained from a Judge and is binding and true. It is legitimized by the laws of good and evil in a court in the highest realm of reality. This law is constitutional, in other words contractual, and ominously authentic in a world of integrity outside judicial fallibility. This is to say that no argument or extenuating circumstance or appeal of mercy has any bearing on its ability to be executed aside from one thing, one clause, one loophole.

There is *only One* possible injunction at the Judge's disposal. It is called Christ's law. On His way to the cross Jesus stated, "Behold, I make all things new." This law is also referred to as the *law of grace.*

With these laws firmly in place and eternally honored, in the foreknowledge of this righteous Judge, this law of grace was implemented as the Son of God left His eternal throne in the halls of heaven to step down into time and space and become one of us in order to amend this contract. In what can be described as original love, Jesus purposed to redeem this warrant, our death sentence, by compensating for its impending penalty Himself.

Only by *accepting* the authority of this bond payment, citing this courageous act, trusting its irrevocable authenticity, and placing Him over this affair in complete confidence, are we then eternally freed from our charge.

Imagine for a moment that I flew you to the moon in my spaceship and once we landed, I said, "You'll have to put on this spacesuit before we can exit the ship." Suppose you asked why this was necessary and I explained that without the protection of the suit, you would die. The temperature of space was such that you would freeze to death, and you would not be able to breath in the vacuum of space without the protection provided by this special suit. Now, you could choose to deny and ignore my warning and decide to exit the spaceship without the suit and put the truth I told you to the test. The problem with this is once you realized I was telling the truth it would be too late.

This is the circumstance with which all humans are faced. Physically, our bodies are not designed to *live* in space. And spiritually, in our fallen state (the nature of our spirit cloaked or tainted with sin) we are unable to live in the presence of a Holy God, who is by nature an opposing force to the darkness of sin within us. His unchangeable nature of purity innately destroys anything less than the complete and utter perfection of His being.

When we landed on the moon, you could have made a different choice. After I explained the certainty of death in exiting the spaceship without the suit, you could *instead choose to believe* this truth, and in *that* case, the fact that I was offering you the protection of the suit would be *Good news!* (In fact, it was *good news* whether you believed it or not.)

When you hear someone say the word "gospel," what is your first impression? What thoughts does this word produce? Gospel simply means *good news!!*

Think of a scenario when you received really *good* news. Maybe your husband lost his job. This is *bad* news, right? In the following weeks, your mind hits the gas and day by day your stress level skyrockets in fear that the bills are piling up. *"What if we lose the car!? What if they shut the lights off!? What if we lose our home!?"* You try to stay positive, but the days and weeks seem to pass quicker than they ever have.

Day after day, your husband returns from his job search in disappointment of the absence of a single prospect. People do one of three things. Impetuously, they fight while blaming each other. They remain silent refusing to talk about it in the hopes that somehow this isn't happening. Or they continue to pray and encourage each other. No matter which way they cope, the reality of a situation like this is taxing to say the least.

Soon, debt collectors have your phone ringing every 15 minutes, pink termination notices cover the dining table, and you find yourself in tears as you hear the familiar squeak of your husband's brakes outside. You wipe your face, so he doesn't see, and prepare yourself for the usual report... but before you hear the front door close, an almost forgotten tone fills the house... "Good news!!!" Your man rounds the corner and scoops you up. "I got the job! And get this, a signing bonus!! Everything's going to be okay!"

This is gospel! GOOD NEWS!!! *This* is what should come to mind when you hear *this* word. *Elation*! Not religion.

The truth is, we cannot survive the glory, splendor or goodness in the presence of our righteous and perfect God, and we are as dead as you would be in outer space without a special suit. We are left floating in a cold, dark place, forever separated from God, without special clothing. But *GOOD NEWS!!! THE* good news!!! The King has saved us. He is our provision and protection. He is our life. The Bible says, "Clothe yourself with Christ." Because *in Him* we come to the Father in *His* light—in *His* perfection. In Jesus' righteousness, we are no longer in opposition to the Father's light. Whether you know it yet or not, this is the *greatest* news you're *ever* going to get!

"But God demonstrates *His own love* for us *in this*: While we were still sinners, Christ died *for us*, since now we have been *justified* by His blood, how much more shall we *be saved* from God's wrath (against the cancer of sin) *through Him*!" (Romans 5:8-9) [inserts mine]

Jesus is our special suit! Notice it says we have been *justified.*

"*Just if I'd*" never sinned.

Peter explains what we've been talking about concerning the darkness in us and God's opposing light; Listen; "But you are a chosen people, a royal priesthood, a holy nation, God's special possession, that you may declare the praises of *Him who called you out of darkness into His wonderful light.*" (1 Peter 2:9)

We can stand before a holy God in the light of Christ *instead* of our darkness. Clothed with our special suit: "for all of you who were baptized into Christ have *clothed* yourself *with Christ.*" (Galatians 3:27)

The next verse says it doesn't matter who you are, where you come from, or what you've done, "For you are *all* one in Christ Jesus." (Galatians 3:28)

God tells us again and again through the Apostle Paul to "Put on Christ." Choosing to believe this truth and trusting that Christ is God's only way to eternal life, we understand that Jesus satisfied God's righteous judgement of sin at the cross. Since He took our sin and darkness, we get to take and have His righteousness—His light.

This made the way for the Father to justify our exonerated souls to enter heaven and live. "God did not send His Son into the world to condemn the world but that the world might be saved through Him." Please get this. I am not at all saying that Jesus saves us *from* the Father; in fact, He saves us *to* the Father, for it was the Father who sent Jesus to reconcile us to Himself. (John 3:16-17)—To bring peace with Him where there was previously enmity. Enmity is defined as "*the state of being actively opposed or hostile to someone or something.*" That *something* is the sin within us.

Be sure you hear me in this though. Just as we understand that we must choose to trust the spacesuit before we exit the spaceship, we must choose to "Put on Christ" and trust Him *before* we exit this world! If we deny the *only* way to life God has made for us, and we choose to put this truth to the test, exiting our life here without Him, once you realize I was telling you the truth, it will be too late. Jesus, Who was God in the flesh, clearly stated, "I am the Way, the Truth, and the Life. *No one* comes to the Father but through Me."

Good news is only good news if you accept it. If the husband, in our earlier story, chose to deny the truth of the position he was offered, and turned it down, neither he nor his wife would have benefited from the offer of that *gospel,* or "good news."

I believe that wife would have desperately pled with her love to accept the good news and take the position offered him. Your heavenly Father, since the beginning, has pled with mankind to do the same. He's called us, drawn us, and engaged in a seduction of His beloved to accept the good news of His Son Jesus and take the position that He offers us in Christ for the greatest of God's purposes... eternal life with Him.

"For God so loved the world that He gave His only begotten Son, that whosoever *believes* in Him shall *not perish* but have eternal life." (John 3:16)

Before Christ came, we were condemned as attached to the affliction of sin, which had to be judged if a God is going to claim to be good. "But now, there is no condemnation for those who are in Christ Jesus." (Romans 8:1)

Again, very GOOD NEWS!!!

Check this out. What do you think it is with these Christians? I mean *really.* What do they have to gain by sharing this with you? What's their angle? Do you honestly believe they need to convince you to be convinced themselves? No, they don't.

So, why go to all this trouble for people... Money? Out of some egotistical need to validate themselves? Really, *think that through*. You think I spend hours out of my days on an ego trip or just to sell books? Believe me; a writer's wage can often be little more fruitful than that of the struggling bit actor waiting tables. And what little my sordid past had left of my ego was promptly checked in God's presence the moment I encountered Him.

Look, I'll solve it for you. Imagine you somehow discovered the cure for cancer. I ask you; would you hide that away in your basement? I mean, what kind of person would do that? No, my friend. This is about the discovery of a lifetime. Hitting the lotto doesn't even touch it. You know, as sure as you're reading this, you've been wondering about it since you can remember. Be honest. And do you know why? Because God placed the idea of eternity within us— a longing for it.

The word of God says that God "has placed eternity in the human heart." (Ecclesiastes 3:11) Did you know that?

I like the next line of that verse. "Yet no one can fathom what God has done from beginning to end." One day I am going to stand in heaven, and I want to see *you* there. That's it! That's really all there is to it. It's called compassion. I cannot stand the thought of anyone going through what I know they will without God. He's shown me. And once you've seen it, you cannot unsee it.

When you come to God, He shows you great and mighty things you do not know. Unsearchable mysteries await you, my friend. When you get hold of the reality of His love for you and how He feels about people you don't even know, well, then *His* agenda becomes *your* agenda. That's the bottom line. I hope you will call on Him and come along for the ride. I promise you; you'll be so glad you did! No decision you will ever make will mean so much or be more significant.

Like a man proposing marriage or a groom on his wedding day, God wants to pull back the curtain and surprise you with something unexpected, something just for you, and who you are. Romance is about attentiveness. It's about paying attention to who your love is and what they care about. It's about understanding their innermost desires. No one knows you like God knows you. No one is more "romantic."

The thing about romance is that it takes seduction to the next level. Romance goes over and above. Romance is extravagant. It can even be a little crazy. More than once, I have let romance take me to extremes.

There was a little road connecting my hometown of Arlington, Texas, to the much smaller town of Kennedale. Kennedale was cool for one main reason, Kennedale Raceway. The small dirt track, about the size of a football field, hosted the amateur and seasoned driver alike. On one end it also offered drag racing. My favorite thing, at the end of the night, was the thrill of the demolition derby!

We lived close enough to the raceway that growing up I was serenaded to sleep by the rising and falling of the distant motors rounding the track. When I moved away from home at 15, I had to adjust to the absence of the soft roaring rhythm. Instead of sheep, we counted laps.

The road I was telling you about wound from highway 287, Arlington's west border, and past an old and very well-kept cemetery named Emerald Hills. There was a patch of road where the trees broke and for about a quarter of a mile you had a clear view of the Kennedale water tower.

The old grey tank towered at about 150 feet and displayed the faded paint lettering "Home of the Kennedale Kats." The small two-way road wound under the tower before one more curve dropped you onto Kennedale's main strip. It was on this corner that my girlfriend worked at a fast-food place named "Burger Box."

One night, while she worked, my buddies and I were having a few cold ones when an idea resurfaced from the day before. We each decided we would meet back at my friend's house and set out for the Kennedale water tower. One by one we returned to my buddy's childhood home laughing at our "get ups." We were all about 16. Each one of us dressed all in black. I had located a stick of eye black from my glory days on the grid iron and covered my face with the stuff.

We loaded my backpack full of an assortment of spray-paint cans from the garage, belonging to my friend's dad. The three of us continued laughing through our attempts to formulate a plan. Our heavy-set pal, Tige (short for tiger) proclaimed our insanity and firmly established he would not be climbing the tower with us. He handed me one of two walkie-talkies and appointed himself "lookout."

Tige drove a sweet, bronze 77 Trans Am. We all jumped in and rumbled defiantly into the night with the spirit of James Dean and the "Magic Power" of "Triumph."

Tige parked on a neighborhood street just next to the tower. Since we already looked like criminals, we moved as fast as we could through a backyard, over a fence, and into the dark field surrounding the tower. It was secured by a chain linked fence topped with barbed wire. I can't remember who brought the wire cutters, but they worked great. In short order we had a hole cut out to squeeze through.

I had to get up on my buddy's shoulders to pull down the ladder extension and suddenly we were on our way up. I will never forget pausing at about the halfway point, looking around and down and then realizing the weight of what we were doing. After reaching the top, I was scared and excited circling to survey our canvas on the railed off walkway. Thought of the thrill on my girlfriend's face fueled me to climb up on the railing, so the message could be clearly seen!

The next day, I made up a reason I would need my girl-friend's car, so I could drive her to work past the tower. I'll always remember, and more significantly, so will she, the moment she saw it. In giant red letters, spread high and wide for all to see, it read "I LOVE (HER NAME)!" Yes, I wrote her name. It was personal. I wanted her to have no doubt it was me. I wanted her and everyone to know the lengths to which I would go to dispel any doubt of my love for her.

Let me ask you a question. Was God created in our likeness or were we created in His? Our desires to express ourselves in this way come from Him. He has gone to the greatest of lengths to dispel our doubts as to His love and devotion to us.

Eventually, the old water tower was retired and taken down, as was the union which sparked the daring deed, but that bold red message still remains planted, however deep, in the mind and heart of the one it was intended for. God has written a timeless and imperishable message in bold red for His beloved. It is intended for *you,* my friend. It says *this* is how much I love you. *This* is how far I will go for *you.*

A decade later, our paths would cross again, this girl and me. Only, she was no longer a girl but a woman. Though a decade had passed, there can be no doubt that the romance which produced a notorious story of rebellious passion had much to do with her willingness to revisit us. Another friend and I were discussing the reunion and the urban legend of the "Valentine Vandals." Suddenly, the fires of a romantic past were stoked, and an abandoned drive-in theatre, just off a major highway, emerged as the memorial target.

Romance can be contagious. People are naturally drawn into its demonstrative nobility. My mom overheard our whispered excitement and when I confessed our intentions to repeat our infamous water tower caper, I was completely floored as she volunteered to help us! *This* was *not* my mother! "You think I never did anything crazy for love!?" she asked.

We loaded up a long extension-ladder in my dad's truck, who was away on a trip to Vegas, and drove into one of the most dangerous areas of Fort Worth to get close enough to an overgrown lot under one of the two old movie screens. Long story short, my mom dropped us, the ladder, and a backpack full of spray-paint, at 2 am, on a dark, dirty street on the southeast side.

She would circle this crime-infested ghetto in the interest of a rebellious romance which had consumed us all. After trudging through the formidable thicket and erecting our 40-foot ladder, I climbed to the top and began shaking the first can of paint. I had not anticipated how this noise would pierce the early morning still.

A flood light from the back yard of a small business broke the pitch-black field and several large dogs began barking. "Hurry!" came a stifled shout. My ambition outweighed the impending interruption, and we heard the squeak of a swinging gate, then the scuffle of the shepherds of the lot. German Shepherds! "I'm out!" my friend announced, bolting away from the closing canines.

I'd barely finished the "I" in "I love you" and slid down the ladder like a firefighter down a pole. I can remember few times I ever moved *that* fast. Leaving the ladder behind, we dashed through an apartment complex and circled back to the street with perfect timing. My mom pulled over and we jumped in the bed of the truck just seconds before a patrol car turned the corner toward us.

The plan was foiled that night but to this day that big red "I" can be seen from I-30 and stands as a testament to radical romance and the extent to which love can propel a heart to act. Romance can indeed be extreme, causing even the most sensible soul to risk all to cement a commitment.

Men have paid to have marriage proposals written in the sky or presented on the giant screens at a sporting event. Some profess their love while freefalling from a plane or even announced by Garth Brooks himself while attending his concert. Romance says, "*This* is how much I love you!" *This* is how high *you can expect* my love to reach. This is how I am different than *anyone* else. This is how much you are *worth* to me!

But romance is not just grand, epic gestures. Often the most romantic signals are sent by way of the little things. This is true because it shows the object of affection that the details of their everyday life, however small, are not only receiving your attention but are important to you.

Ask a woman whether she would appreciate a grand gesture once a year, and little attention in the meantime, or daily attention through intimate gestures in lieu of the annual hoopla.

I believe you will find the latter is unanimously preferred.

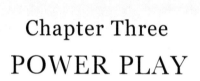

Chapter Three

POWER PLAY

"The man who is most aggressive in teaching tolerance is the most intolerant of all; he wants a world full of people too timid and ashamed to really disagree with anything." ~Criss Jami

The valley we visited earlier shows two dynamics at play—grand, yet intimate. There is a story which tells of both ends of the romantic spectrum as well. It is as modern and current as the last few minutes, as it is ancient and eternal. This story is arrayed with the grandest of risk-taking sacrifice and the most personal and minute exhibitions within the tiniest details. It is timeless and boundless on a scale of life and death, and as seemingly trivial as casually implemented favors in our daily routine.

All the way through the annals of history, God has conveyed a romantic seduction in a phenomenal choreography of music and dance in His relentless pursuit of mankind. He could have chosen to reveal Himself to us in any number of ways. We can imagine a deep booming voice quaking the earth beneath us. Or perhaps, if we were Him, we might make our entrance in some magically royal presentation of light and dramatic sound while surrounded and engulfed in an angelic wave of blue fire and golden chariots.

This imaginative revelation, though powerful *and possible*, would instantly intimidate us as well as alienate us from believing we could relate with Him. No, God chose instead to walk through our lives with us, breathing His wisdom under our pens in unrivaled poetry. Patiently helping us understand Him *and* ourselves, He wove Himself into every possible story of His creation so that when we read it back, we would see His guiding hand, His loving heart, His faithful and reliable vows. We would see Him *beside* us.

His understanding, mercy, forgiveness, strength, and grace would not be distantly separated as He towered over us in condescending pity. But instead, would kneel right down beside us as our familiar Brother, as our Friend, as our doting King. He has not chosen to lord His greatness over us as something we could never aspire to. He has come down to us and entered our weakness, our pain, and our desperate condition to lead us out of it by showing us how to come up to where He is, yes. But *even more*, that we would become like Him, and then *even more*, be *one* with Him.

He came to show us that lordship, in His kingdom, is servanthood.

He *is love* and the King of love. Love is sacrifice.

In John 6:44 Jesus tells us, "No one can come to Me unless the Father who sent Me draws them, and I will raise them up at the last day." Remember the word "seduction" means "To draw aside to one's self".

The genius planning of the epic romance known as the gospel of Christ is as simple to the spirit as it is a mystery to the natural mind. This seductive courtship lays down a brilliantly romantic powerplay of poetic and boundless wisdom which dwarfs any other to convince the most rebellious heart in an unparalleled devotion and all-out, irreversible commitment, leaving no possible doubt as to its genuine authenticity.

Jesus said, "Greater love has *no one* than *this,* to lay down one's life for his friends. You are My friends if you do what I command." (John 15:13-14)

Maybe the person you love would lay down their life for you. We want to believe they would. The only way to know for sure is if they were placed in a position where that kind of commitment was actually put to the test. Your God was put to that test. Jesus was God who became a man for this purpose. He not only proclaimed His love and commitment to you but proved it with great suffering and death for you.

The most convincing part of the truth of His love is that He did this knowing exactly who you are and asked for nothing in return except for you to recognize His love as true and believe in Him. Have you ever had anyone else who has done this for you?

Anyone else. Let's talk about someone else who vies for your affection, who calls for your respect and time, your loyalty, your trust, your belief. Yes, you are special, and your devotion means more than you may think. There is another suitor, another "lover", who pursues you. He too has thrown his name into the hat as a candidate for your hand in marriage. He can appear very attractive. In fact, he is a prince and, at times, even an angel of light.

As will mortal men in their efforts for the conquest of your heart, he will question the sincerity of his romantic rival. He has gained a lot of experience with this tactic.

In reality, he has been employing this strategy, among others, with great success since the beginning of time.

"Now the serpent was craftier than any... He said to the woman, "Did God really say, 'You must not eat from any tree of the garden?'" The first woman (Eve) answered saying they were told they could eat of all the trees but one, and if they ate from that tree they would die.

"You will not certainly die." said the serpent.

This reminds me of two guys that may typically be "after" a certain girl. You have the guy your parents like, right? He is the clean-cut star athlete who loves his mother and volunteers at church functions. He drives a Honda, holds a 3.8 GPA, runs for class president, brings flowers for your mom, and even helped your daddy replace the alternator on his truck.

Then, there is the dark and mysterious long-haired dude dressed all in black, with the nose ring, who tosses rocks at your window and offers a ride in his flame-covered muscle car at 3am, while casually flicking his cigarette butt into the bird bath.

And which one do you think this girl is more taken by? It struggles to make any sense, but our default attraction almost insists we explore the darker places, to find excitement in danger. Why do you suppose this is true? It not only alludes to the conditional truth of the intrinsic darkness of humanity, but indeed, validates it.

This picture is a hypothetical scenario, but I am willing to bet that you have played one of these three roles at some time in your life. If you were either the "nice guy," the "bad boy," or the "princess," you may have very little problem with a sympathetic understanding of at least one of them.

For a brief moment though, even if you're not yet a parent, step back from your familiarity with any other character and place yourself behind the eyes and in the heart of the mother or father of the "princess." Honestly ask yourself which one of these two boys you would choose for her.

The crazier thing is that this "bad boy" treats your "princess" with arrogance and indifference and is blatantly apathetic toward either choice she might make. It seems he could take her or leave her and would be as unaffected by her protest as by her interest in him. In the meantime, Mr. "Nice guy" falls all over himself to provide for her every trivial whim and openly professes his indestructible love and devotion for her. Our human nature and propensity longs more for the thing that most eludes us, no matter how insubstantial its value.

The intangible unknown is as tantalizing as the certainty of stability is boring. That is, until you grow up! And until you understand that fantasy and fact dictate their own individual rules and there is a vast chasm of difference between knowledge and wisdom.

Every day, through the knowledge of science, physics, mathematics, history and philosophy, this dark prince attempts to discount anything outside the parameters of knowledge. The one variable, unaccounted for, is the unseen or unknown. Knowledge, by definition, is "The known."

For instance, before certain discoveries, there were things that fell outside the realm of knowledge simply because they were yet unknown. The microbiological world of DNA, subatomic particles, quantum physics and the accelerating expansion of space were not included in the accepted sphere of knowledge not long ago. Does this mean they did not exist before they were discovered? Of course not.

It is assumed there is an iron clad agreement within the scientific community that until something is proved, in that it transcends mere theory to become "absolute" by undeniable evidential fact, it remains speculation. However, this is not the case concerning the theory of evolution—it is philosophy, not science.

In light of recent revelations, it takes more faith to believe in this idea than it does that of intelligent design. Though still unproved by innumerable problems which continue to increase, Darwin's *theory* has been printed and presented as fact in curriculum textbooks and force fed to generations of gullible students in every classroom.

Darwin himself stated that if, by way of future technology, it could be proven that life's evolvement was not the result of progression in small increments, his theory would fall apart (more on this later). Indeed, an elementary dive into currently accepted microbiological data-fact fulfills his prophesying disclaimer. Not to mention the absence of a transitional fossil record.

You see, when you are young, the unknown is intriguing, and your mind is open to all possibilities. As you age, these mysteries move from excited expectation to excruciating aggravation. The unknown becomes uncomfortable, and the human mind or *soul* has a crippling necessity to place certain things into a box it can organize and file under the heading "Conducive" —Conducive to what I *need* to believe—Conducive to the size of the box I've prepared—Conducive to my abhorrence of the idea of eternal accountability—Conducive to the freedom I enjoy within the lifestyle I choose to live.

Conducive is defined as- *"making a certain situation or outcome likely or possible."* There are things that can be fashioned to become conducive to a particular purpose, and there are things that, no matter what the effort, will never be conducive to certain purposes. That "bad boy," who is trying to seduce you, wants to confuse the two.

There is a term called "artistic" or "poetic" license. The mortal employment of the term emerged around the middle of the 19th century but has been a useful strategy in Satan's playbook for eons. If you are not familiar with this term, it is "the freedom to create an artwork, musical work, or piece of writing based on the artist's *interpretation* and *mainly for effect*. Artistic license often provokes controversy by offending those who resent the *reinterpretation of cherished beliefs* or previous works." (Dictionary.com)

The enemy of all things good has a plethora of tools or methods at his disposal. Perversion seems to be his favorite and incorporates many of life's essential venues. He successfully applies "artistic license" to, of all things, *truth*. One of the most effective techniques is known as offense. Offense is brought to the surface of the mind and then conversation when certain expectations go unfulfilled. This "artistic or "poetic" license employed by evil draws on the fallen nature of humans to present illegitimate expectations cloaked as legitimate, even virtuous, necessity.

Its premise suggests that simply being human *must* afford us rights that support our own individual preference of *whatever* truth we choose. No matter how ludicrous, it assumes the preference valid simply because everyone should be entitled to live out *any* truth.

The pretense of their assumed "virtue" states it to be inhumane to offend anyone's personal belief even when it seeks to remove all borders of morality and confuse the obvious natural order of the world, i.e. as a society, we should not only allow and condone the 60-year-old man living as an 8-year-old little girl, but indeed, should applaud its courage. With all that truly strains our world today, there are millions of people and several organizations that simply seek to push the line as far as they may with no thought of consequence.

I would suggest in what is referred to as "the interest of inclusion," by people known as "progressives," there is no perimeter of reason applicable to, or even on the horizon of, the mind of this movement.

This ought to terrify you!

This is literally the "bad boy" with a bag full of drugs and a box full of condoms secretly plotting to coax your 12-year-old daughter through her bedroom window and out into the night. He has used a counterfeit license with a bold letter heading of "Tolerance" to present a "reinterpretation of prior works and cherished beliefs" to offer up a perverted proposal disguised as compassion.

This proposal has been swallowed "hook, line, and sinker" by an "entitled" generation who is marketing anyone in opposition to it as racist bigots or some other label usually ending with the suffix "phobic."

The irony lies in the fact that fear (phobia) is at the root of offense in that they are in fear their expectations of some twisted, all-inclusive utopia would go unfulfilled or be thwarted by "old-fashioned" and "sensible" conservatives. Now I'm guilty as charged of the afore-mentioned sensibility, because my hope would be that the "nice guy," the star linebacker, would ride in on his white horse, or even his Honda, and save my naïve daughter from the illegitimate proposal while effectively laying a hurt on her perpetrator that he won't soon forget.

Listen folks. God is offering us that service. But as I said, we want *more* the thing that eludes us. The grass is greener, right? In this case, it appears greener because it is fake! It is artificial turf. All that is presented to us by this rebel kid is just that, ingenuine. His ultimate goal is to transform us into the phony reinterpretation of authentic truth. To place his dark, refitted cloak of compassion on us for one reason, to duplicate himself, to build his coalition of counterfeit crusaders, and to parade us down the streets of glory as his rebel clone's, in a march of mockery before the King who banished him.

If you want the Truth, then step right up! First and foremost, *grow up!* North is still north, south is still south, up is up and down is down. The sky is blue, the grass is green, light and darkness are opposing forces, oil and water do not mix, and what goes up must come down. Males are males and females are and always will be females. Right and wrong are opposites and as I've said before, truth cannot be manipulated without disqualifying itself as truth. It is not relative and does not yield to anyone's opinion of it. Regardless of anyone's attempt to repackage it, the validity of truth stands alone with or without your compliance.

In the event that the daughter (princess) in our tale chooses the brooding boy in black over the pining prince of purity, this ill-advised action will never negate the "nice guy" as the *right* choice. Neither will the attempt to pervert the wisdom of God's eternal law, by even a vast majority shouting loud enough and long enough of offense or perceived injustice, have the least success in this futile endeavor. You may explore space, but you will never traverse it. You may sail the seas, but you will never calm them, and you may climb Everest, but you will *never* move it.

I'll grant you that choosing the "nice guy" may not be as thrilling in contrast to what you may imagine of the "bad boy," but recognition of right (knowledge) and the decisive act of choosing right (wisdom) will ultimately avoid destruction and produce stability, security and subsequently peace, which inevitably brings happiness. This principle, though obvious on the surface, is reserved for the matured mind. Immature minds see it in theory, but the wise mind acts on its truth.

You do not have to abandon common sense. And one does not need to agree with someone or condone wrong behavior to be compassionate. Right and wrong will never succumb to a society's willingness to compromise their borders any more than the light of the sun will be prevented from shining. You may well lock yourself away from its light or create clouds of deceit to obstruct it- but it shines on still.

As I've stated, Christians don't relay the message of Jesus because they have some egotistical need to be right. Nor is it to be condescending to anyone or point a boney, judgmental finger as if to say, "You'll be excluded!" (If you have experienced this, it is ingenuine.)

There is one reason *true* Christians are compelled to share their faith. Correction, two. We are commanded to, and we care. The compassion of our Lord to save every soul and the power of His supernatural transformation of our lives dictates that to hoard this truth would be the most heinous of cruelties.

Jesus said, "Whoever listens to you, listens to Me; Whoever rejects you rejects Me; but (Know this) whoever rejects Me, rejects *Him* who sent Me." (Luke 10:16)

"If people do not welcome you, leave their town and shake the dust off your feet as a testimony against them." (Luke 9:5)

The love of God is such that it will not be forced on anyone. Though His heart breaks for those rejecting Him, He will not force them to believe Him. Forced love is not love at all. Why secular society insists on being offended by the non-threatening message of Christianity is beyond me and seems completely unreasonable until you consider its motive and opposition. You will not be hunted down or your personal character publicly shamed; You will not become the target of hate crime from any true

Christian, as is the custom of other religions that the secular community supports!

If you choose not to believe, then go your way in peace. But ask yourself, if there's nothing to it, if Christianity is not the truth, then why are so many offended and bent on bringing it down? And why has this been the case for millennia?

Our enemy comes to "steal, kill and destroy..." He is stealthy. If you haven't noticed, the root word in stealth is "steal." He is the "bad boy" who sneaks up close to your window in the middle of the night. The greatest deception he has ever performed is in convincing the world he does not exist.

I believe, as bad as Lucifer longs to be worshipped, he is smart enough to know that to completely reveal himself would shine a light on the spirit realm and so, expose God as well. No, for now, he is perfectly content, and oh so patient, to stay in the shadows lest he give away strategy. At times, his agenda shines forth quite brightly. The bible says he has the ability to portray himself as an angel of light.

This agenda surfaces as a noble quest to include any and all forms of wickedness or else cry foul in the spirit of "freedom." It displays right and wrong as relative terms and slowly desensitizes our youth to see evil as common and casual parts of everyday life.

Hitler, who embodied the spirit of anti-Christ, was given a revelation by this dark prince, a vision of strategy. He saw clearly that in order to accomplish a genocidal agenda against God's chosen, he would need the hearts of the youth in the land. He understood how vulnerable and impressionable they were and sold them a cause and an individual purpose in which they could find their identity.

The human spirit is innately searching for a purpose and a truth in which to belong. This drive is common to every human being. It was born in Eden and has survived the fall as a built-in device in search of a Beacon. That Beacon is the light of the world, who is Christ. As I've said, there is one who seeks to intercept this inherent appetite. To do so, he disguises himself as light on a path to "truth" which offers itself a "deliciously appealing" supplement for humanities eternal hunger.

Hitler managed to infiltrate young minds to the point they so believed in his cause or "truth" that they would loyally turn over their own parents to be murdered by him. There is a similar spirit at work in the minds of young Americans today which has been gradually slow cooked in hell's kitchen for generations. Its main ingredient prepares other hereditary elements grown in Eden's garden—rebellion, selfish pride of entitlement, and a victim mentality (Or offense). Patiently allowed to simmer until the table is perfectly set and the ambiance carefully orchestrated, this stew is seasoned with ancient spices that have successfully served its wicked chef from the gallows of Pharaoh's Egypt to the gas chambers of Adolf's concentration camps.

Indeed, the much more obvious persecution of moralities' militia comes from the outside in the form of Islamic oppression, but this is in coordination with a growing internal cancer known as inclusion. If somehow it can be shown that inclusion is universal to any idea and all exclusionary thought a representation of bigotry, then the stage is set for the "Grand Opening" of the chef's buffet. We must understand the battle being waged for the hearts and minds of our youth and take our stand for them no matter what label they themselves choose to attach to it.

> "For nation will rise against nation, and kingdom against kingdom... and *you will be hated by all nations for My name's sake. And then many*

will be offended, will betray one another, and will hate one another. Then many false prophets will rise up and *deceive* many. And because *lawlessness will abound*, the love of many will grow cold." (Matthew 24: 7, 9-12)

"You will be hated by *all nations* for *My name's* sake." Why do you suppose this *one truth* will be hated by the whole world? Why do you suppose it is hated now, as we speak? There are a lot of religions, many opinions of truth. What's so special about this one that, in a world which cries out for inclusion and tolerance and promotes "relative truth," this particular one is singled out as unacceptable?

Verse 10 through 12 above say, many will be offended, will betray, and hate one another. (Followed the news or social media lately?) Then we're told that many false prophets will show up on the scene and deceive much of society. A prophet is someone who dictates what's coming in the future. The next verse says that lawlessness will abound. In other words, clear lines and established moral borders will disintegrate or decay in the interest of inclusion and obsessive sensitivity to offending views. Anything not viewed as all-inclusive or tolerant will be rejected. Tolerance becomes intolerant to one thing, the truth of Christ.

The prophecy of the last book of the word of God (Revelation) tells us what this world will look like. One world government and *one world religion*. This is the main course of many being served up from hell's kitchen.

The story is told that on one occasion, Vince Lombardi's team was told they would have to share the team's locker room at a road game they were scheduled to play. One of his assistants entered the room where Lombardi was preparing his strategy for the game.

The assistant quickly closed the door for privacy and dropped a book folder on the coach's desk. When Lombardi was told that the opposing team had inadvertently left a copy of their playbook in one of the lockers, he abruptly slid it into the trash can. This action pictures genuine integrity and rare character.

There is one playbook however, we should study with fervor and resolve. Its strategic prowess is as fiendish and lethal as it is artful and accommodating.

> *"Throughout history, it has been the inaction of those who could have acted; the indifference of those who should've known better; the silence of the voice of justice when it mattered most; that has made it possible for evil to triumph."*
> *Haile Selassie*

In psychology, desensitization is a treatment or process that diminishes emotional responsiveness to a negative, aversive, or positive stimulus after repeated exposure to it.

The desensitization to the boldness of societies' progressive depravity is, to me, more shocking than the symptoms themselves. These evils have always thrived in secret, smuggled along in the dark web of the human mind.

As tolerance becomes the slave of offense and inclusivity claims its place on the ladder of virtue, it relentlessly pulls down shame on its way to the top. Shame then falls on the head of objective morality to scold it as bigotry.

Truth, by definition, is exclusive. Therefore, it no longer finds its place in this "progressive" coup which, almost unwittingly, poisons itself drinking the waste society produces while bingeing on the buffet of unrestrained relativism. The entrée, once seen as absurdly unpalatable becomes a delicacy and opens the collective mind to the possibility, even probability, that there is nothing that should not be considered acceptable or delicious, no matter how minimal the collective endorsement.

In its extreme evolution there is required only the individual's absurd idea presented under the virtue of inclusiveness to establish a reasonable validity. Otherwise, all ideas would need scrutinization and be subject to rejection, and rejection is the enemy of tolerance. With the premise of this "virtue" comes the conclusion that everyone should be allowed to openly display, express, and promote any idea, no matter how wicked the proposition. The end of this concept's progression is the verdict that nothing is inherently wrong; and that evil is simply any suggestion in favor of exclusivity or absolute truth.

While reading the story of Noah and the flood, I used to question the fairness or reasonable justification that society had become so totally and irreparably evil to such an extreme that it would be necessary to destroy it completely. That is, until I seriously began to consider the above-mentioned progression in our current day.

> "Then the LORD saw that the wickedness of man was great on the earth, and that *every* intent of the thoughts of his heart was *only* evil *continually*. (Emphasis mine) and the Lord regretted that He had made man on the earth, and He was grieved in His heart." (Genesis 6:5-6)

Once this train reaches its inevitable destination, God will judge.

James saw this progression in terms of the life of sin. "Then, after desire has conceived, it gives birth to sin; and sin, *when it is full grown*, gives birth to death." (James 1:15)

As sin is fed, nurtured, and allowed to grow healthy and strong, it breeds more sin. Like the individual, our society is two dogs- one white and one grey. As society feeds the grey dog of subjective morality, it starves the white dog of objective morality until eventually objective morality dies leaving no opposition, no alternative to depravity—nothing to stand in the way of evil. So that, just as in Noah's day, the thoughts and intents of all mankind are nothing but evil continually. This conducted piece of wicked brilliance will crescendo when the true followers of Christ are raptured, taken up and out of this world and the restrainer of evil, the Holy Spirit of Truth, goes with them. There will no longer be anything to counter prodigal living in those who have rejected Christ and no memory of the truth of good.

When that which now restrains evil, namely the Holy Spirit in the hearts of God's saints, is removed, the cancer of evil will consume all remnant of good, leaving only the hunger and thirst for ever increasing forms of wickedness.

Failure to slow this "runaway train" will see the Captor's foot fall harder on the throttle until any attempt to obstruct its velocity will be futile, even deadly.

"Bad men need nothing more to compass their ends, than that good men should look on and do nothing."
~John Stuart Mill (1867)

As offense prevails in the social arena, it bleeds into the courts, and as the rock of established law shatters under the weight of the chisel of compromise and the hammer of tolerance, it weakens with every blow. Complacency and cowardice shadow the diligence of the righteous and the shovel of subjective morality digs an ever-deeper pit.

Moral decline is in overdrive and the fact that so few are sounding this alarm supports the point that as the sun gradually sets on objective morality, the eyes of even those in opposition have adjusted to the absence of light. Here in lies the most dangerous element.

Good men and women must act now. We must gather our numbers, organize, strategize, and boldly resist the licentious militia. We must identify the specific dangers, make our cases, recruit, and elect those who will fight with us. We must pray; for the battle must first be won on the spiritual front or no victory can come. As air forces are sent in to soften the warzone for advancing troops, we must bombard our enemies' fortifications on bruised knees. We must also bravely and aggressively engage the physical front and advance to take that ground in the social arena of our world. We must be willing to leave our pews and ruthlessly war to conquer with intelligent campaigns of reason, logic, and historical evidence. To spotlight not just the murder of morality but that innate and fainting recognition of *right* in every human heart.

We must appeal to what is already evident and raging to escape the conscience and rally behind the inveterate cry of the human spirit for justice, for decency, for good and for naturally common sense. We must be willing to shout loud enough and long enough of the approaching plight of our children and future generations.

Two plus two still equals four- for now! This is in our favor! But if we allow a more committed minority to consistently refute the existence of an absolute truth, we will lose vital ground and sink into a complete and total Orwellian existence in which "four" becomes a customized composition of subjective, unrecognizable digits.

We cannot continue to be the patient who is in denial of his diagnosis. The subtlety of this enemy is such that he introduces a bacterium which may seem harmless at first glance.

The ability for bacterium to cause disease is what is known as pathogenicity. The bacterium our enemy has introduced is *inclusivity*. *Tolerance* is the pathogenicity (the means by which) inclusiveness can cause destruction (disease). And *offense* is synonymous to what is called virulence. Virulence (offense) is that which provides a quantitative measure of the pathogenicity (or likelihood) of causing disease (destruction).

Before I lose you, my point is that imbalances within the body determine whether certain individual elements become a sickness. The elements in and of themselves may not be harmful but in quantitative measure (levels of imbalance) they become difficult for the body to fight. Left unchecked this difficulty increases until there are not enough good cells to fight the corrupted ones.

You see, *offense* is almost undefinable. Because it must be recognized as an individual, personal feeling. In other words, anyone must have their unique feeling of offense validated, as there is no tangible way of disproving its existence or extent independently of the heart of the one who has been offended.

So that, by default, every position taken in offense must not only be noted but affirmed, reconciled, and then compensated. And any resemblance of protest against the offended, perceived as insensitive, is instantly labeled as generically phobic and crude. In the plethora of phobias currently used to expose "bigotry," I can imagine "ideophobia," or some other propped-up shaming mechanism, will characterize anyone even questioning the sincerity of someone's proclaimed offense.

Then, as long as someone claims to be offended by even a particular statement (free speech), that speech will be labeled "hate speech." This campaign is gaining ridiculous strides as you read this book and it would not surprise this writer to find this book banned as soon as a decade from now. Artwork is already being removed from the public square in the name of offense and the return of book burnings would logically follow suit.

Oh, how very clever our adversarial genius—to cunningly introduce this insidious pathogen into the bloodstream of society and patiently wait for its cancerous effects to ravage our moral structure and destroy the hope of mankind.

Satan knows well that the Word of God is mankind's only cure. If he can convince the world that it is hate speech, the world will then reject the remedy for its demise.

> *"Woe to those who call evil good and good evil, who put darkness for light and light for darkness, who put bitter for sweet and sweet for bitter." (Isaiah 5:20)*

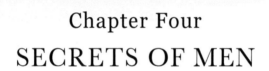

Chapter Four
SECRETS OF MEN

"Truth is not a matter of opinion, or the justification of that opinion, or the ability to persuade the masses. It is a mountain which needs only the wind of humility to remove the cumbering clouds of duplicity." ~Patch Spears

People discuss everything from occupations to sports, "good old days" to dinner plans, and when that awkward silence hits, there is always the subject of the weather to break through the pause. But do people ever *really* talk? I mean about the "big" things they often ponder late at night while the spouse sleeps and the TV garbles twenty different sounds into a buzzing distant distraction.

There are some particularly important, profound things we should be talking about. The truth is people do take the time to bring the "heavy" issues up. Unfortunately, by and large, it is not until they reach their death beds.

I wish I could remember all the details of conversations I've heard, and even had, in the last days of the lives of people I've known.

It's sad, I can recite every word of the classic song "Stairway to Heaven" but I have a hard time recounting the most important words the people closest to me had to say. That may ring a morbid tone but, in those moments, people set aside speaking their minds and truly, often for the first time, speak their hearts.

Have you ever sat in a hospital room with someone who was dying and just instinctively commented on the weather? Any other time, they would have taken the handoff and followed with, "Crazy huh? They say it's supposed to warm up though!"

Instead, they display a look that seems to stare right through you as if they missed what you said. In reality, they didn't miss it at all. But we are no longer where we used to be. We are not in the days when sports or the weather or the price of tea in China matters at all, are we? In these moments, on this day, those topics hold no value whatsoever. They are a waste of precious breath and very expensive time. Out of obligation, in the weight of irrelevance, and for pity's sake, they turn toward the window and nod over a listless grin before returning to the query of their heart.

So, you sit quiet, in a cloud of insignificance, helplessly unable to rise above such superficial sentiment. This is simply because we never took prior opportunity to do so. A hard thing to convey in words but even if you haven't been there *yet*, you will be. We must get that when we reach this page of our book, our occupations, the playoffs, the approaching cold front or who won American Idol are no longer detectable on our mind's radar.

Oh, some people are thick skinned enough to pretend to be engaged in these subjects and even sing a defiant declaration song of satire for the "grim reaper." While inside them, the deepest of issues and emotion are raging to get out.

As people approach the finish line and the last few pages begin lifting off the back cover of their book, they want to know what's next. Is there a next? Could heaven be real? We get up every day to our routine and though this question frequently passes through our minds, it is tragically and abruptly set aside to make way for the present call of the task at hand. This "can kicking" might continue for a lifetime but when we are suddenly faced with the reality of death, it becomes an all-encompassing exercise in speculation, wonder and fear.

Often, while skimming the surface of our lives in conversation with people, I feel the prompt to bring the true issues of our existence onto the boat. Most people quickly seek to avoid such subjects and either excuse themselves or nervously divert their willingness to confront such depth. This dereliction of effort to dive deeper reveals the most catastrophic consequences in respect to the time that is forfeited or squandered with our children.

Their inexperienced, uncorrupted, and fertile minds are open and willing to be taught, but these time sensitive and formative years are crucial and fleeting. We tell ourselves we have plenty of time. We teach them about life, what is right and wrong. We may take them to church and even hold regular Bible study. But often we think the *deep things* of God should be left to God. So, we file certain things we've learned to be true about Him under "personal relationship." We then deny them the benefit of our wisdom. God does not do this to *us*, nor should we do this to our children.

Somehow, we think deep discussion will alienate our children or maybe make them think certain secrets of God to be *weird*. Many times, it's simply because we feel our own knowledge to be inadequate to answer tough questions they may have, and we're afraid that if we don't have the answers, it will affect their faith... or ours.

By admitting our limits and showing them where and how to find answers we are not only equipping them to seek truth but ensuring they won't think they are some oddity, "less than," or somehow unworthy when *they* don't have all the answers.

One of the most surprising lessons of life is the contrast between our initially apathetic view of time and the actual speed in which it moves. Whether aware of it or not, as you read this book, you hold a view or idea of the time you have left in your day. Unless, like me, you read to get to sleep, you probably have a plan for the remaining hours. In the same way, you have an idea of how long you might live and certain hopeful plans to fill those days. Whether people admit it or not, they carry an underlying, albeit presumptuous, confidence in their remaining "years."

Just as *this* day will end much quicker than you suppose or just as the last five years have surprisingly slipped by, you will land on the doorstep of eternity, and it will seem as if *no time* has passed between then and now. Ask anyone who stands there today, and they will affirm this truth. When it all comes down, there is but one unavoidable question every person must ask themselves. Do I believe this life is all there is... -or not? If you have yet to answer this question, maybe these two questions will help.

Why should I believe? Why shouldn't I believe?

If you will take these two questions seriously and exhaust all efforts to answer them, resolving to employ every resource to do so, I promise, you will find your answer. But, as Lee Strobel urges, "Make it a front burner issue in your life."

If you're already a believer, in respect to our children, I'll urge you *and myself* to refuse to take the preciously productive years of innocence for granted. "Train up a child in the way they should go and when they are older, they will not depart from it." (Proverbs 22:6)

My mother was no theologian, but she consistently drove one thing home. With regularity she stressed the importance of truth and that Jesus loved me.

She would say, "The ugliest truth is better than the prettiest lie." This idea of the importance of truth echoed off the walls of my mind and was a constant, if often ignored, companion as my life unfolded. As truth always does, it circled back to knock on the door of my heart time and again.

I wonder if you'll try something with me. Perhaps you've questioned God's existence or have believed for a long time, or just recently placed your faith in Christ. Whatever place you find yourself today, let's set all doubt aside for a few minutes and assume God *is* real and that indeed Jesus is the only way to get to heaven. Now, imagine you have come to the last 24 hours of your life. Nothing can be done to change this. In just 24 hours you *will* leave your life in this world. Let's say, to your shock, an angel has just visited you and revealed these truths to you.

Again, this may be tough for some to completely absorb but play along. Assume that unequivocal proof has shown you that Jesus is the way God has provided to live forever in heaven, and that anyone without belief in Him will be eternally separated from God and His paradise. Now, you have 24 hours left to do what you will with this truth. What is your response? What will you do or say with undeniable confidence in this revelation?

No one's asking you to fully understand it, just that it *is*. What I want to do while you consider this is answer the other perplexing enigma you may not even realize you're facing. *Why, amidst all other possibilities in the realm of human reason, does this one idea ring out louder, clearer, more authentic and naturally solid than any other!?*

The word of God answers this question. It says that God "has given to every human the measure of faith." (Romans 12:3) "He has made everything beautiful in its time. He has also *set eternity in the human heart*; yet no one can fathom what God has done from beginning to end." (Ecclesiastes 3:11)

God is in the business of giving people hope, not condemning them. He has placed faith in eternity with Him inside your heart so that when we hear this *Truth,* we know in our hearts it belongs to us— even as the enemy tries to convince us to reject it. The choice you have is not whether it's true or not. The choice is whether you will receive the power of it into your life right now. Look, God is going to judge evil and punish it. Believe me, this is the God you want; not one who would let evil off the hook and so condone it. If God, Who is the source of all good, and its defender, does not hold evil accountable, then who will?

If given just 24 hours to do and say anything I wanted, I hope I would help anyone and everyone I could understand the truth they've already been prepared to hear and may not have. It's plain, but listen with your heart, will you?

> "For the wrath of God is revealed from heaven against all ungodliness and unrighteousness of men, *who suppress the truth* in unrighteousness, because *what may be known of God* is manifest (recognizable, apparent) *in them,* for *God has shown it to them.* For since the creation of the world, His invisible attributes are clearly seen, being understood by the things that are made (creation), even His eternal power and Godhead,

so that *they are without excuse*. Because, although they knew God, they did not glorify Him as God, nor were thankful, but became futile in their thoughts, and their foolish hearts were darkened. Professing to be wise, they became fools." (Romans 1:18-22)

Not only has God placed the ability to recognize His truth, and a hunger for it within you, but He has displayed Himself plainly in the world around you to the point that these two things leave you without excuse to ignore Him.

As is common, there may be those who will read this book for one reason. To "review" it for the purpose of "suppressing the truth." As the first lines of the 18th verse above reveals, they do so in ungodliness and unrighteousness because, even to them, God's truth has been shown. They are not thankful for this truth but have become futile (fruitless) in their thoughts, their foolish hearts darkened by the evil one, and though they will profess to be wise, they are fools. Romans goes on to say that in accordance with their hard and impenitent (remorseless) heart, they are treasuring up wrath for themselves in the day of wrath and revelation of the righteous judgement of God. (Romans 2:5) *(author's paraphrase)*

Understand, there is no partiality with God. He loves and seeks to redeem the darkened and foolish heart that scoffs at His very existence as much as He does the one who is sincerely and openly considering Him.

And please get this my friend; it is not the hearers of the truth that will be justified by God, but the doers, the receivers of His gift. There is a difference between believing *that* and believing *in*. This recognizing hunger within you will be the very thing for which you will be held accountable. He speaks of the Gentiles (those who don't yet know God), who still by human nature do the things in

God's law (instinctively knowing right and wrong). Even though they do not attribute this to God, they are accountable to this which God placed within them. (Romans 2:14) (paraphrase)

> "...who show the work of the law (truth) written in their hearts, their *conscience* also bearing witness, and between themselves their thoughts accusing or else excusing them in the day when *God will judge the secrets of men by Jesus Christ,* according to my gospel." (Romans 2:15-16)

What I am trying to help you realize is the thing which you already recognize as truth was placed within you for this very purpose. It's no accident that this puzzles you, even bugs you to a point. We were created with a need to answer this question, to find what fits in that empty space inside us. You will never be able to cram anything else into it. Not a lover, not alcohol or drugs, or any other earthly thing. Satan will try very hard to convince you that you can, but until you receive the piece that was created to fit that hole, you will miss it and the peace that comes with it.

There is a part of you, created in the likeness of God, that judges right from wrong, truth or lie, and that very part will hold you accountable under the revelation of your own suppressed convictions; Or will be exonerated by your faith in the One Person who could and did receive the penalty of righteous judgment by a good and Holy God over all evil forever.

The key to this truth is to understand that no person is righteous and the whole world is guilty before God. Until you understand this, you will not understand our need for a Savior. This is why, *without Him,* we will be judged on our merits which can never measure up to the perfect standard of God. "All fall short of the glory of God." (Romans 3:23)

Just look at it this way. If you *are* the darkness in a room with no light and God is the brightest light bulb you can imagine, and that light was suddenly turned on, what would happen to you as darkness? There would be no you any longer. It is impossible for light and darkness to simultaneously occupy the same space.

This is us in heaven without our faith in Christ. It is just as impossible for good and evil to simultaneously occupy the same space. God knew this would be the case before He created the world. We are, as it were, a damsel in distress. But not just any damsel. We are His beautiful bride to be, "the love of His life." "God *is* love." (1 John 4:16)

So, how would He save His bride and completely convince her of His everlasting love for her?

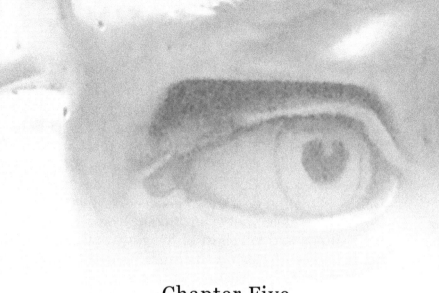

Chapter Five

A DARING RESCUE

⁓

"Love recognizes no barriers. It jumps hurdles, leaps fences, penetrates walls to arrive at its destination full of hope." ~Maya Angelou

The gospel (good news) is to understand that good (which God is) must hold evil accountable. A righteous God would not be so if He did not judge and punish evil. We've seen that God judged all evil at the cross and laid its punishment on Jesus so that He could have mercy on us and pardon us. The only way we can escape judgment and punishment for our unrighteousness is to acknowledge this mercy's pardon for us through the truth that Jesus satisfied the punishment brought on evil at the cross of Christ.

"Therefore, by the deeds of the law (doing enough things right) no flesh (human) will be justified in His sight, for by the law is the knowledge of sin (so we understood right from wrong). *But now*, the righteousness of God *apart from the law* is revealed, being witnessed by the law and the prophets (foretold by them); even the righteousness of God through faith in Jesus Christ, *to all and on all who believe.* For there is no difference (between anyone). For all have sinned and fall short of the glory of God, being *justified freely by His grace* (unmerited favor) through the redemption that is in Christ Jesus, whom God set forth as a propitiation (payment) by His blood, through faith, to demonstrate His righteousness, because in His forbearance (predetermined mercy) God had passed over the sins that were previously committed, to demonstrate at the present time His righteousness that He might be just and the Justifier of the one who has faith in Jesus." (Romans 3:20-26)

In plainer English, God had given the law, so we would be clear on right and wrong, but no one could refrain from enough bad nor do enough good to be justified in the sight of a perfect God. So, God revealed in Jesus how He would be able to be both righteous in judging evil and merciful to us *who believe* by making Him the payment for our sin through His blood on the cross.

Also, it makes no difference who you are, because there is no one who could ever be good enough on His own. And to *all* (anyone) a justification before God was freely given, *by grace*, through the fact that Jesus has redeemed us. God decided beforehand in His love and mercy to justify *anyone* to live with Him in eternity who has faith in Jesus. I believe, from all we know, that a conversation something like this could have taken place.

With evil's deceitful victory in the garden, an ominous darkness settled over the earth. There was solemn silence on the Holy Mountain of heaven. Angels knelt in honor as the Ancient of Days spoke with the Son:

"Our man has come to the day of his fall. He will surely be lost without that which he owes. My hand has been lifted against them in righteous judgment and My Word must be accomplished."

The Son replied: *"As I am Your Word, I will accomplish and fulfill it. Our love will see evil conquered as Your right hand crushes Me in their place. Righteousness will be satisfied and by grace Our love will be manifest."*

The Father: *"Then I will honor this thing in that I exalt You above all, in judgment as King, and all who will call on Your Name, I will honor as justified by the same, and acquitted for Your Name's sake. For You have chosen and I have commanded this decree; that henceforth there will be no condemnation to those who believe on Your Name for that which this sacrifice accomplishes.*

That by descending Your throne to stand in their stead for the fulfillment of righteousness to preserve the eternal integrity of My Name, You will be appointed the Truth by which all may have eternal life. Of which I have purposed and now sworn to by My Merciful Name."

As a massive wave of the roaring waters of this decree rushed forward throughout eternity, the message came into the moonlit room of a young girl. As the regal angel Gabriel spoke, by faith she answered, "Let the will of my Lord be done unto me according to your Word." And that night, in the fulfillment of time according to this world, the Holy Spirit of God brought the eternal King of the universe into the womb of a teenage girl.

The most wonderful love story the world would ever know began its final chapter. As the Son of God lay in the frailty of a human infant child, a multitude of angels praised God saying, "Glory to God in the Highest, and on earth peace, good will toward men." God's Will sent peace in reconciliation with Him, toward mankind, in His only Son.

The enmity (state of active opposition) which resulted from man's disobedience in the garden would be overcome and forever reconciled in the obedience of His Son. This mastery of man's great mistake was manifested, as the God of all mercies placed Himself at the mercy of the hand of the very man He created.

Since the hour of man's fall from consonance, God had been preparing him for the time He would enter our world. (Genesis 3:15)

"With the Lord a day is like a thousand years and a thousand years are like a day." (2 Peter 3:8)

So, through our millennia or His *days*, His Spirit revealed to Godly men the truth of His Son's miraculous entrance into time and space, and this Son was made known as the "Christ," "Messiah," or "Chosen One." During this time, the enemy of God and man, the condemned and banished fallen angel called by many names, sought to destroy the bloodline of Adam born into the nation of Israel.

His efforts to thwart the plan of God are revealed repeatedly throughout our history. Recognizing Jesus as the promised Son of God (or Christ), Satan employed every available resource and opportunity as he salivated in excitement that finally he would destroy God's eternal plan to rescue man from his rule.

He stood by in delightful braggartry, with his wicked wingmen, as the whip scattered flesh and bone from the body of Christ. *"My day has finally come! The hour of my victory is at hand!"* Satan ranted.

I can just see him reclined on a bed of flies at the foot of the cross, his snout raised in anticipation of the sweet scent of death. As Christ speaks His last words in pain, "Tetelestai!," we can imagine a dark grey fist raised high in triumph by the dark prince.

This Greek word used is translated to English as, "It is finished!," and rings out through history as the sign that man's sin is forever defeated, and the power of death broken. However, much of the significance of this statement is lost in this translation.

"Tetelestai" means to bring to a close, to complete, to fulfill. As Columbia International University's website states, and I quote:

> *"What makes this exclamation truly unique is the Greek tense that Jesus used. (Verb tenses are the most important and most communicative part of the Greek language. This also is sometimes necessarily lost in translation.) Jesus speaks in the perfect tense, which is very rare in the New Testament and has no English equivalent."*
>
> *The perfect tense is a combination of two Greek tenses: The present tense, and the aorist tense.*
>
> *The aorist tense is punctiliar: meaning something that happens at a specific point in time; a moment.*
>
> *The present tense is linear: meaning something that continues on into the future and has ongoing results and implications.*

> *"The combination of these two tenses in the perfect tense, as used in John 19:30, is of overwhelming significance to the Christian. When Jesus says, "It is finished." (or completed), what He is actually saying is, "It is finished and will continue to be finished." ... In conclusion, in Jesus' statement "It is finished," we have a declaration of salvation that is both momentary and eternal... We are ransomed from the kingdom of darkness and then, we confidently rest in the reality that "it will continue to be finished" because we are in a position of grace and stand justified for all time before God."*

I can almost see Satan's expression drop from glee and then morph from surprise to squinting query, then, into that "thousand-mile stare" of shock and disbelief.

"What is He saying?" are the words that hang themselves in the window of his twisted mind until Christ is raised to life, and defeat's bitter realization brings a nausea the likes of which the angel of evil had never known.

Like the victorious Hero leans into His mighty horse, rearing up in silhouette before the setting sun, King Jesus speaks His final orders clearly before ascending the clouds to take His throne again at the right hand of the Father. Now, in His resurrected body, He commands His rescued bride: "Go into all the world and preach the gospel (good news) to all creation. *Whoever believes* and is baptized *will be saved*, but *whoever does not believe will be condemned."* (Mark 16:15-16)

Your bride is in a burning building. You bring a giant net, many men, and stand ready just under her window. "Jump honey! We'll save you!" She has two choices. Believe, jump in faith, and be saved. Or, do not believe in you and the way to safety and she, by her own choice, will be condemned to death. She has one way to be saved, but she must believe that this is the only way if she is going to be saved.

You have been rescued from drowning in the depths of the ocean. Your saving boat has pulled up beside you and the rope has been tossed to you. Will you now be so arrogant and ungrateful as to complain about the color of the boat? Or worse, will you be so blind as to insist you are *not* drowning?

I know what it is to be dying and vehemently refuse any help. I became so submerged in a bottle that, as Eric Clapton once said, "The only reason I didn't kill myself was that it would mean I could no longer drink."

Sometimes hope has eluded us for so long we come to believe it was never there in the first place. It's like being locked in a pitch-black room where you cannot see your hand in front of your face. You grope around in the darkness in search of the light switch. After enough time goes by in this effort, it becomes monotonous and then pointless as you plop down on the bed convinced now that this room never had a light switch to begin with.

With hope, the weakest of men can do the greatest of things. Without hope, the strongest man in the world can't even pull himself out of bed. If the bed is your ultimate goal for the day or perhaps the bed *is* your day, I'm here to tell you, no, I promise you, there is hope my friend. There is always hope, the greatest of hopes, and His name is Jesus. He has not just rescued you from death and into His paradise, but He has rescued you for a purpose right here, in the now, in today. I know you may think as I once did, you are just too far gone, and the way back will be too long.

This is the devil's lie.

In fact, you will be surprised just how close to good and complete restoration you really are. He traversed the cosmos for you. He endured more excruciating agony than any man will ever be able to contemplate—for you. Do you really think that depression or addiction or heartache is too much for Him to overcome for you? He overcame death itself. And His resurrection purchased more for you than you will ever be able to fathom on this side of eternity.

He is in the business of bringing dead things back to life. That's what He does, and He does it oh so well my friend. Take one step toward Him and He will show up and show off in your life. The building is burning, and He is there with His net. The sharks may be closing in around you, but His boat awaits you. Grab the rope. Call His name. Allow Him to rescue you and hold on tight, because He flies quite fast at times. You will break through those thick, dark clouds and into the sunshine. Soon you will say with me, "He is my Rescuer! He is my King! He is my Lord!" And as crazy as it may sound coming out of your mouth, you will say it! "He is my Friend!"

Listen. Forget religion! A friend of mine has a shirt I love that says, "My relationship won't allow me to have a religion." Men have a tendency, indeed, a bad habit, of mucking things up. This is to say they complicate things and just can't leave a good thing alone. For some frustrating reason they feel the need to "improve" something when no such necessity presents itself. "If it ain't broke, don't fix it!"

This rescue is not your U.S. Navy dropping you off in a safe zone from a war-torn country with a salute and a "Best of luck" assertion. It's not your tight fitted government servant patrolling the neighborhood of your life in search of some violation of regulation. No, this is the One Who made you, Who knows why you are the way you are and isn't the least bit surprised by who you are.

This is the One Who knows you better than you know yourself which, by the way, is why He is the only One qualified to help you. By all accounts, in every way, and on every day, He *is on your side*. So, by His decision to obligate Himself, by His own Will, to *be on your side*, and bound by perfect integrity to sustain you as a visible pillar within His character, He will, at times, allow some things to walk through your life that are tough to swallow and even tougher to figure.

Though gaining the wisdom He holds for you or having the likes of patience produced in you can often be abrasive, the love of God will never allow that which is not for your growth, strength, and ultimate good. If you were completely convinced of this principle, you would never stray from Him. Since many of us are not convinced, we grab the wheel and seek to deliver ourselves from a storm which He has intended for us to endure for His good purpose toward us. In reality, God's intent is to reveal something about Himself to us, while our mind's bent is to view it as punishment.

Understand that to grab the wheel from Him is to place our lives in *our* hands, under *our* control, and so produce results within the limits of *our* power and ability. Or we can trust Him to drive and enjoy the results of unlimited power and ability.

"Now unto *Him who is able* to do exceedingly, abundantly, above all that we ask or imagine according to the power that works in us..." (Ephesians 3:20)

"He is in all things working them together for the good of those who love Him and are called according to His purpose." (Romans 8:28)

Read that verse again and then remember this one, "For I know the plans I have for you," declares the Lord, "plans to prosper you and not to harm you, plans to give you hope and a future." (Jeremiah 29:11)

Now that sounds like a rescue to me! If you simply got a hold of the truth within these three verses, your life would be forever transformed for good! This amazingly, brilliant thing God has done for you is for one reason, He loves you and wants you with Him in eternity, that's true. But He wants you near Him *now*, and to reveal all that this nearness brings to you. "Call to me and I will answer you and show you great and mighty things which you don't know." (Jeremiah 33:3)

So, let's get this straight. God creates us to live forever with Him. We blow it because we were deceived by an evil angel. This sin prevents us from being near God, so that there is no way we can go to heaven with it. It's passed to every human because you cannot inherit something from your parents they don't possess. Adam no longer possessed the sinless nature He once had.

We can't fix it because the consequence of sin is death and must be paid for with death. God came to the earth as a man named Jesus to rescue us and do for us what we cannot do for ourselves. God must judge the evil of sin, because good must hold evil accountable, and God is good. So, in their love for us They (the Trinity—Father, Son, and Holy Spirit) formed this plan in eternity past, with foreknowledge of this impending dilemma. Jesus would live the sinless life forfeited by Adam and stand in our place to satisfy the requirement of a just God. As an *innocent* Man, Christ's *voluntary* sacrifice gained the power to override our death penalty and return us to our original position in right standing once again with the Father. Brilliant! *This* is the good news of Christ. *This* was a daring rescue indeed.

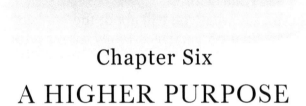

Chapter Six

A HIGHER PURPOSE

"The ultimate test of a man's conscience may be his willingness to sacrifice something today for future generations whose words of thanks will not be heard." ~Gaylord Nelson

I had cause to say to my twelve-year-old son, "We need to talk about something." He's become, like many his age, enthralled with a game called "Fortnite." It's easy to see why. When I was a boy, we were just being introduced to this enticement. I first began playing video games around the same age in the late 1970's but they were quite simple in retrospect.

"Atari" produced such games as "Asteroids" and "Space Invaders," and I can remember being captured by them for a time. However, they didn't compare with our own imaginary adventures while traipsing through the countryside of my uncle's farm and the hundreds of adjoining acres. We created worlds where we were cowboys and Indians in epic battles or an army battalion fighting Nazi and Japanese foes attempting to take over the world.

Other times, we accurately played out our roles as James T. Kirk, Mr. Spock and the crew of the Starship Enterprise as we imagined our surrounding landscape to be some distant planet which we'd all landed on to "seek out new life and new civilizations" and "boldly go where no man had gone before!"

You can say what you will about the "violent" nature of such imaginations, and it certainly supports the discussion in favor of a "fallen" world to observe these innate tendencies, but, they are what they are. Kids inherently enjoy this timeless portrayal of themselves, involved in an adventurous conflict against a perceived evil, with them as the heroic righter of wrong. Couple that with our natural inclination to compete and, in young men in particular, but not exclusively, you will typically notice the essence of these types of behaviors emerging.

Had I reached my twelfth year in our current day, and discovered a game like Fortnite, I likely would have lost my mind in its adventurous world, just the same. Kids today have little need of imagination when someone else's suffices so well. In the thirty-seven years since I was my son's age, our technology has indeed seen some amazing leaps.

Without wisdom, we dive into the apparent benefits of modern abilities- barely glancing at an assessment of what it may cost us socially. What character developments are being sacrificed in the individual, family, and societal realms?

Social media allows us to connect on a wider scope, with more people, more regularly, while creating a less personal and practical connection. As a "fly on the wall" at any family function, we witness everyone sitting in the family room, "together," but checked out of that moment, opting instead to be mesmerized by whatever is being streamed into the device in their hands.

Device- regardless of your world view, the word's origin and plurality reveal irony. I suggest it even exposes purpose. Their definitions, taken together, reveal much.

"Device" comes by way of Old French "devis" based on the latin, "divis,"or "*divided*," from the verb "divider." The original sense was "desire or intention," found now only in "*leave a person* to his or her own devices." (This has become associated with "sense 2.")

More common in the current vernacular, the word is associated with phones, tablets, laptops, games, PC's, TV's etc.

First definition- *device*; a thing made or adapted for a particular purpose, especially a piece of mechanical or electronic equipment—gadget, utensil, contrivance, or *tool.*

What I want you to see is how the second definition works strangely in tandem with respect to the first.

Second definition- *device*; a plan, scheme, or trick *with a particular aim*—ploy, tactic, move, stratagem, plot, ruse, maneuver. The irony is outstanding.

In the video game "Fortnite," a player is dropped into a bordered world where the goal is to collect resources, eliminate other players, and be the last one alive. It is very similar to the idea portrayed in the best-selling books and feature films that are "Hunger Games." Following a growing concern facilitated by a substantial increase of time that Noah spent playing this game, I informed him that I would be implementing a policy of "balance" with all "devices." After I placed a reasonable daily limit of "game time," he proceeded to his room, slamming the door in protest.

I quickly and dramatically entered his room to express that this attitude and behavior would not be tolerated. He's at the age that intrinsically seeks to test the boundaries he may be afforded, and I was all too committed to revealing exactly where those borders stood as well as the impenetrable solidity with which they were fortified— Basically fulfilling my least favorite part of being a dad.

Our relations with God are perfectly synonymous. Like our own children, we will seek to test the limits of God's grace. Though there are no such limits He may choose to apply to our lives, we assume we can manage this dispersion under our own limited wisdom. God has bound Himself by one all powerful force concerning us, and that force is known as love. The form or path this force desires to take is the one of least resistance. However, its greatest ambition is that of a good and fruitful outcome in the life of the *loved* one.

Isn't this our approach? Where it is obvious that pain and *only* pain will produce such an outcome we maturely and naturally, though somewhat grievingly, allow it to have its place and proven effects. We refer to it as "tough love," right? Our nature since Eden has been to rebel against good in favor of that which we believe will create adventure, fun, or some physical or emotional pleasure.

The juvenile human mind forgoes the possible, even probable, negative consequence of tomorrow for the temporary satisfaction of today. Often the circumstances of rebellion aren't as significant as the act itself. Sometimes the excitement of going the wrong direction is sufficient satisfaction on its own. The conventional or status quo seems boring. As kids it places us in a box with "grown-ups," and as adults, it restricts us to a mainstream, which we see as unsensational, lacking fulfillment.

Why is it that our adrenaline levels rise at the very thought of impropriety?

What if I suggested that the "taboo" thing was nothing more than a strategic "device," employed by our enemy, who does so with a perfect understanding of the nature he so cunningly coaxed us into to begin with?

Why is it that most people live their lives with full comprehension of the necessary boundaries their children require- knowing them to be good for their ultimate happiness- but then disconnect themselves from this wisdom in relation to their own circumstantial borders?

These parent's practical behaviors completely contradict the common sense with which they instruct their children. Incidentally, and appropriately, they practice this nonsensical, hypocritical, refutation in the skeptical gaze of their children because they, themselves, were careful to study the same contradiction in the lives of their own parents. "Do as I say, not as I do," right?

This philosophy is rationalized as credible in the minds of parents everywhere, even with me. After all, it "worked" for our parents. It *never* "works," because children observe that these rules are time sensitive. As soon as they are of age, they think it not only their privilege and rite of passage to cast them aside but, indeed, to take up the same conflicting dynamic with respect to their children.

An equally important by-product of this deviate, two-faced, directive is how it is translated with respect to our willingness, dare I say *ability*, to trust God. How should they perceive Him as any different than our parents or other adult influences who strictly command and encourage one lifestyle, while blatantly living out another? Even if, by some miracle, they believe what you've told them about God, or anything for that matter, subconsciously their view of truth is impaired.

Subsequently, for them to accept the truth that God's Word holds complete integrity, in that it is impossible for Him to be contradictive, will become a much tougher mountain to climb mentally, emotionally and practically. It will be much more natural for them to place your truth about God into a file beside all your other contradictions.

One scripture in particular has become quite sobering to me as I've considered my careless dereliction in this subject. God takes very seriously our responsibility with the innocence of our children. While speaking specifically about children, He stated, "If anyone causes one of these little ones-those who believe in Me- to stumble, it would be better for them to have a large millstone hung around their neck and to be drowned in the depths of the sea." (Matthew 18:6)

We all make mistakes. We are much better parents to allow those mistakes to work for us rather than against us when we own up to them instead of attempting to cover them through impotent rationalizations. For when this "cover up" approach is utilized, its strategy is then adopted by our children to justify their own rebellious endeavors. By owning our missteps, we bring them into the light and expose them as erroneous, shoring up our credibility and simultaneously removing rationalization as a valid means of living. We remove the grey matter and draw clear lines of right and wrong which will serve our precious children in the most crucial choices they will face.

Every minute we sit in our children's presence, our faces aglow with the light of our phones, teaches them that *this* is acceptable social behavior, *this* is the norm, *this* is what's important.

I am not making news to say that devices divide. There is one who seeks to conquer society and he begins with the family. In those where he can successfully drive out the father and separate a family physically, he does so. If this scheme fails, he is crafty enough to separate the family inside the home by taking their attention away from each other.

The most successful strategy ever implemented in war is to "divide and conquer." In more modern times, the "prince of the power of the air" has put the space between satellites and his victims to "good" use for his purposes. There is power in numbers, and as he triumphs in separating our numbers, those purposes come to fruition.

Our children grow more and more distant. Our friends become nothing more than a Facebook feed and pictures on a page. And even as our families reunite on holidays, they have never been more personally disconnected than while sitting right next to each other!

Don't misunderstand. I am no more immune to this than anyone else. As I write these words on a Saturday morning, my twelve-year-old plays his game and my ten-year-old follows the upcoming NFL draft on ESPN. An hour ago, I told them we would play "Monopoly" at the dinner table in about fifteen minutes. So that we don't fall victim to any more time apart, time I'll one day wish I had back; instead of using how long it takes to finish a game of "Monopoly" as an excuse not to play, I now feel inspired to spend this entire rainy day at it.

Remember, *romance* will "draw aside to one's self." It is not reserved exclusively for the "lover" or just for God. If you have children in your house right now, or a spouse who is otherwise engaged, this might be the perfect opportunity to *romance* them...

So, after a six-hour game of Monopoly, I realized, there are countless teaching moments it presents. More importantly, we had more laughs in that six-hour board game than we had the last month combined. This, my friends, is romance, and it was priceless.

Romance must be intentional, folks. Romance is little more than quality time, taken intentionally and thoughtfully. It is making the sincere effort to carefully gather those things which are important to your loved one and incorporate them into a conversation. That conversation is not always displayed or accomplished with words.

There is a poetry that surfaces and permeates undistracted time shared in an experience which is about nothing else but the one you love and what means the most to them. Every moment we complacently forfeit, while hypnotized by our devices, is forever lost.

Catherine Booth (1829-1890), co-founder of the Salvation Army, once said, "In order to better the future, we must disturb the present."

"The best use of life is love. The best expression of love is time. The best time to love is now." (Rick Warren- *The Purpose Driven Life*)

God created us to belong. We have all done things when we were younger, and maybe even recently, to belong, or fit in. When I was twelve-years-old, I had to attend summer school so that I could progress to the eighth grade. One morning, after the bus had dropped me about twenty minutes early, I noticed a very attractive girl, standing across the street, smoking a cigarette.

She was a couple of years older than me and I bummed a smoke from her, just so I could talk to her. Three minutes later, she walked away and crossed the street, leaving me spinning in a nauseous stupor that robbed me of the ability to stand and promptly had me stretched out on the side of someone's house for the next hour.

This choice, the briefest of moments, barely a period at the end of a sentence, in some way altered my destiny. In a small paragraph in time, on a scarcely significant narrative page, in what later became an otherwise forgetful chapter in the book of my life, this brief lapse in judgment was the catalyst to thirty-five years as a smoker. Ironically, what seemed so very trivial to the story, placed a giant question mark over how many pages might fill my final chapter.

I wanted to belong. Regretfully, I did belong, in a life-long attachment to a very costly and unhealthy habit. Our love for our children strives to process these tough life lessons into productive measures to prevent our kids from making such choices.

We talked about bringing our mistakes out into the open and the benefits of that practice. But a very thin line must be walked as we instruct our children and determine what scope, or to what extent, our mistakes are exposed. Often, as I previously mentioned, our errors are used by them to rationalize their own actions, rather than heed them as legitimate warnings.

One child believes they'll receive your approval by conforming to your exampled admonition, while the other may see it as an opportunity or "pass" to test the waters of rebellion and affirm their identity as a subconscious way of relating or connecting to you. Both siblings are groping for a way to belong in relative association. One, in relative compliance. The other, in relative defiance.

Once again, the spirit of this aspiration is hardwired into the heart of humanity. Frequently, rebellion is little more than an experiment in stability. It attempts to test the strength of the harness that secures us to someone. This is not only acted out by children, but by immature adults suffering from insecurity. Insecurity is fear, and it promotes an irrational perception of one's own worthiness. It is a paranoia that promotes a self-preserving manipulation of truth for the purpose of controlling an outcome they believe will dispel their imagined fears, or, at least, give them some sense of control.

Proverbs 9:10 tells us, "Fear of the Lord is the beginning of wisdom." The word used there in the Hebrew language is "yirah," or "yare," and means "moral reverence," or "awe." Another word translated as "fear" is "phobos," (from which we get the word "phobia") means "terror," "fleeing panic," or "alarm." This kind of fear is not of God. It is the primary weapon of our enemy because its effective implementation directly contradicts and cancels out faith. Jesus repeated one phrase more than any other- "Fear not." In fact, God has been saying this from the beginning. There is no fear in perfect love. (1 John 4:18)

The reason this is true is that true and perfect love is *complete* trust. There is no love without trust and when trust is complete, there is no fear. This is the crux of faith, the pillar of belief. The Bible says that we love God because He first loved us. When we experience this love, we then love. We cannot genuinely love God until we are in complete confidence and possess an undeniable revelation of God's love for us. This is where true faith begins to thrive because once we are aware, undoubtedly, of God's perfect love toward us, we then realize that, because He is all-powerful, nothing can happen to us outside of His allowance. We can then have true faith which is obedience. Belief and obedience are inseparable. When we believe something, we don't just say it; we *act* as if it were true.

Jesus was asked by His disciples, "What must we do to do the works God requires?" Jesus answered, "The work of God is this: to *believe* in the One He has sent." (John 6:28-29)

Jesus said, "Anyone who loves Me *will obey* My teaching. My Father will love them, and We will come to them and make our home with them. Anyone who does not love Me will not obey My teaching. These words you hear are not My own; they belong to the Father who sent Me." (John 14:23-24)

Our highest purpose is trust. It is what God seeks most from us, and if you'll think about it, we want the same from our children. Trusting God and reflecting His character toward our children to produce that trust from them are our highest priorities.

The Holy Spirit wrote through Paul that "Love never fails." Now, we know that he was not speaking of human love, because it often fails. Paul was writing about the love of God. (1 Corinthians 13:8)

God is integrity. It is impossible for Him to lie. (Hebrews 6:18) Paul said, "We have this hope as an anchor for the soul, firm and secure." (Hebrews 6:19)

"He is not a human that He should lie or change His mind." (1 Samuel 15:29)

"For no matter how many promises God has made, they are "Yes" in Christ. And so, through Him, the "amen" is spoken by us to the glory of God." (2 Corinthians 1:20)

Then Paul writes that with faith in Christ we have a guarantee. "Now, it is God who makes both us and you stand firm in Christ. He anointed us, set His seal of ownership on us, and put His Spirit in our hearts as a deposit, *guaranteeing* what is to come." (2 Corinthians 1:21-22)

When we promise our children something, we do everything in our power to deliver on that promise, don't we? Though our intentions are true, and we fully intend with all integrity to keep a promise, circumstances can occasionally arise which are beyond our control, and we can be forced to "make it up to them."

Our heavenly Father has no such limit on His power and ability to overcome any circumstance to deliver on His promises. So, the question then becomes, "Will He?" rather than, "Can He?" This is where perfect love comes in. The Lord is an anchor to our soul that is firm and secure. He has promised that when the "whale of opportunity" swims by, and we fail to recognize, by chasing it, we are being led into a raging storm, then, His Holy Spirit within us guarantees His anchor will hold us firm and secure.

Just as our children trust in us to employ our wisdom on their behalf to protect them, we trust in God for the same. Our highest purpose, as parents, is to honor the trust our children place in us, even when they don't understand it. This is our nature because we were created in God's image and His highest purpose is to honor His word and our trust in it. "I will honor those who honor Me..." (1 Samuel 2:30)

As I've said before, our children must be able to trust us with their innocence and naiveté. God wants us to trust Him in the same way.

I remember what it was like when I would worry about things. Stressed to the limit, I must've been a sight. I wish I could explain with words how freely at peace it is to refuse to worry. Don't get me wrong, I'm not saying that I don't experience adversity, troubles, problems or pain. The difference in me today is I know there is purpose in these things, and they have been allowed for my growth and maturity in the faith.

> "For the Lord corrects (disciplines) those He loves, just as a father corrects a child in whom he delights." (Proverbs 3:12 NLT)

When I think about how much I love my own children and how, even when I botch it, my actions come from a place of love and aspiration for their good, I then realize that God is perfect in this way. He not only gives and takes away from me with a heart of perfect love towards me, but He is infallible to this end. Wise above comprehension, yes. Loving to me, *personally*, without measure, yes. Knowing all that will ever happen in infinite detail, yes. But all-powerful, all-capable and all willing to mete out the greatest of integrity for His glory and my good in every single tiny corner of my existence! This knowledge is peace my friends. True peace. The peace which surpasses understanding. Yet, He allows me to understand it in every way I need to right now.

Proverbs 3:13 states, "Blessed are those who find wisdom, those who gain understanding." He would not have said this if we were unable to have it.

This is the trust of a child. Your child may not always like it, but he trusts that you know better, and you do. When your child obeys and loves you anyway, you are pleased. Jesus said, "Truly I tell you, unless you change and become like little children, you will never enter the kingdom of heaven." (Matthew 18:3)

Did you know you can enter the kingdom of heaven here and now? As we submit to the love and wisdom of God, and trust Him in every circumstance, no matter how painful or confusing, by faith we release His power. We then receive His peace over those trials to produce the manifestation of His perfect will in our lives. This is the ultimate victory.

"So, anyone who becomes as humble as this little child is the greatest in the kingdom of heaven." (Matthew 18:4)

'For everyone born of God overcomes the world. This is the victory that has overcome the world, even our faith." (1 John 5:4)

Chapter Seven

TOUGH LOVE

~◯

"The pattern of the prodigal is: rebellion, ruin,
repentance, reconciliation, restoration."
~Edwin Louis Cole

Imagine you were hopelessly, head-over-heels in love with someone. If you have never experienced this, then I pray one day you will. But, for now, you are going to have to rely on the stories or examples of others. If you have children and they are your everything, in that you would die for them, then you can use that context here.

Now, imagine, the person who has your love not only had no feelings for you, but were disrespectful, hateful, and even cruel toward you. Some of you can relate, as I can, to loving someone who you knew were completely dependent on you for their survival, even if they weren't aware of it. Literally, that if you were not there to help them, they would destroy themselves and everyone around them.

Let's take it to an extreme so that we see the object of our devotional and sacrificial love currently engaged in actions that will eternally destroy them and others we love as deeply. This is a desperate, frustrating, and heartbreaking scenario. They will not listen to you, and you cannot just stop loving them. What do you do in this situation? You must, as mutually painful as it will be, allow them to hit bottom.

Sometimes, that can take a while, and the easier we make it on them, the longer it takes for them to reach this point. We call it enablement. The opposite of enabling is employing what we call "tough love."

Tough love realizes the talking is over.

Tough love steps back and allows the one we love to suffer the consequences of their actions.

When we read of the punishments imposed by God, revealed in the Old Testament, we can see them as harsh or unloving. In reality, they are acts of love in order to bless and produce good when all other tactical attempts have failed—to turn God's people away from destruction.

It's strange, but we completely acknowledge the legitimacy of tough love within our own relationships and criticize its productive and acceptable qualities with respect to God.

There is nothing on this planet more complex than the human brain. But the more complicated something is, the more ways it can go wrong.

One of the most certain ways our minds can go wrong is when consequences for bad behavior are removed, intercepted, diluted, or diminished.

Far too many parents today are more interested in being their child's friend than teaching them the rules and regulatory standards of society, both legally and socially.

You can say what you like, but the fact is lack of discipline, and the traditional family unit's role in the intended balance to implement constructive discipline, is wreaking serious havoc in the current and emerging generations. I concur with a vast populace in the belief a devastating void of understanding has been created in the vacuum left by the rapidly increasing number of secular and sinister minds to insist on the all-out eradication of God from every crevasse of the globe.

Love, as we've discussed, can be the greatest motivator for positive change. It propels us to accomplish almost anything. In fact, when fully embraced, *in truth*, there is no unreachable good. "With God, all things are possible." (Matthew 19:26)

The wisdom of love will recognize sometimes pain and loss are necessary in order to bring about restorative good. It is incontrovertibly evident throughout history; it is humanity's nature to take good for granted. Someone has said, "When you take things for granted the things you are granted get taken." Another well-known observation is, "The definition of insanity is to continue in the same behavior, while expecting a new or different result."

The most unloving action would be to allow the ones we love to continue going down a road we are certain will lead to their destruction. Failure to exhaust every effort to turn them around and prevent this tragedy, accurately defines us as unloving.

> "My brothers and sisters, if one of you should wander from the truth and someone should bring that person back, remember this; whoever turns a sinner from the error of their way, will save them from death and cover a multitude of sins." (James 5:19-20)

When encouraging words of love fail, pain becomes the greatest agent for change. No one moves so quickly away from the fire as when they fall into it completely. When we enable someone's error, we are effectively taking their hand and holding them from falling into the fire. They remain at just enough distance from it to see its beauty and feel its warmth while discounting its danger. Some people will remain so mesmerized at the fire's edge as to deny its power to destroy them.

While in this state of deceitful dissent, the fringes of their life become singed and then scorched. The bridges of relationships, career, and health collapse into ash heaps all around them. Fixed on the glow of the fire, they are oblivious to the growing desolation surrounding them.

To remain in this place, sustained only by the enabler's "damage control" will eventually see their life's opportunities in complete ruin. Before that happens, and in order to prevent total devastation, we must let go and allow them to feel and fully experience the truth of the fire they seek to embrace.

This is distinctly what God will do for us. Notice, I said *for* us, not *to* us. We can find tough love on display throughout the annals of God's Word, but what is revealed in the book of Hosea clearly shows us the heart of God in this matter. A broken-hearted God who has expressed His willingness to remove His hand from His children's rebellious existence to accomplish two things.

One, to reveal what their lives would be without Him. And two, to prevent their behavior from the totality of its ultimate and complete repercussion. He loves us too much to allow us to sink so deep into sin that we reach a barren state in which we have lost everything, including hope. How much of our lives we see destroyed depends on our willingness to continue suffering loss rather than turn around and call on the One who willingly seeks to save us from it.

> "No temptation has overtaken you except what is common to mankind. And God is faithful; He will not let you be tempted *beyond what you can bear*. But when you are tempted, He will also provide *a way out*, so that you can endure it."
> (1 Corinthians 10:13)

God knows where your limit (bottom) is, and though that bottom may include losing every earthly thing you have, His purpose in this is to show you life's ultimate value in eternity. God can restore any monetary or physical possession, but without protecting and securing your soul for His heaven's eternity, these things are meaningless. Jesus said, "For what shall it profit a man, if he shall gain the whole world, and lose his own soul?" (Mark 8:36)

You see, there is a danger, a law dynamic in the spiritual realm which dictates when we play with "fire" or engage in the ways of darkness, we are fair game for the "prince of darkness." This is his territory, his realm of authority, if you will. Since God rewards our obedient and honorable trust in Him, He cannot reward our rebellion, lest He condone it. Again, "I will honor those who honor Me, and I will despise those who despise Me." (1 Samuel 2:30)

The integrity of God's goodness will not allow Him to condone evil. Many want to live their lives without Him until they need Him. It does not work that way. If you choose to ignore God, you are entertaining, inviting, even embracing Satan. Jesus said, "You are *for* Me or *against* Me." (Matthew 12:30)

"If you choose not to decide, you still have made a choice." Using this truth and a familiar analogy, if you are stranded adrift in the middle of the ocean and a boat sails by, you may choose not to die in the ocean but if you do not choose to get on that rescue boat, you are, in fact, *choosing* to perish.

That boat may or may not sail past you again before you die. Every time we notice the Spirit of God sail past us, attempting to flag us down and offer salvation, is one less opportunity we have to grab the rope and choose to accept our Rescuer's offer.

One day, that ship will sail past and away from our procrastination for the very last time. Then, the moment we leave this world, we may scan the horizons for it, but tragically, it will be gone. How many times has that ship passed by you? How many more times do you expect it to?

The uncertainty of life for the next year, or week, or even the next hour promises nothing. You could set this book down, walk out your front door and have a heart attack. Or you could be one of the forty-five thousand people who die every year on this nation's highways. You could simply lie down to sleep tonight and never wake up. These are not pleasant thoughts, but the reality is this very moment may be the last time this ship's opportunity passes you.

"All those who call on the name of the Lord *will be saved*." (Romans 10:13) Call on Him, won't you? When the last ship sails, it will be too late.

This is the ultimate reason God continues to allow pain in our lives. Honestly, I think, more times than not, it is the pain of futility. In other words, "spinning our wheels".

The person who continues to reject God relives an increasingly monotonous cycle of impotence and hopelessness in which it seems they are always swimming against the tide or walking into the wind. One step forward, two steps back will wear us down to the point we do one of two things; cry out to God in our brokenness and receive His restoration, or curse Him in bitterness and get back on the treadmill of vanity, only to start the cycle process all over again.

Imagine, for the sake of this correlation, you were like God, and could see the future. Let's say you saw the only way your child would learn certain truths, truths that would prevent disaster, was by enduring hardship. For the greater good and to build strength and character, which would bring favor, fulfillment, and protection in a life filled with joy, he or she must face specific adversities. Without these hard lessons, they would live a life of misery and eventually self-destruct.

Having the benefit of this foreknowledge, would you then spare your child these trials? True love recognizes when tough love is necessary. True love takes the heartbreaking measures required to see their loved one overcome the obscurity of immature rebellion to move into the clarity of restoration.

God chose to reveal something amazing to Hosea by sharing a relative pain. He brought Hosea into an intimate understanding of the broken heart of God for His people. Can you imagine how breathtakingly powerful it must've been to know the Creator of the universe would trust you with such intimacy? Or such intimacy could even exist? Can you fathom how surprising and overwhelming this revelation was for Hosea, to realize how similar God's heart was to his own? He would never see God in the same way again!

God told Hosea to go take for himself a wife of harlotry (an adulterous wife). (Hosea 1:2)

At first glance, this seems to fly in the face of God's directives. In reality, God was revealing an intimate part of Himself with Hosea, and subsequently, with us. He immediately gives the prophet the reason for this command. "For the land has committed great harlotry by

departing from the Lord." (Hosea 1:2) In the very beginning of these declarations to Hosea, He also reveals that
He will save them in His mercy, after the consequences
of their rebellion.

Once "tough love" had its desired effect and they
return to God, He promises that "in the place where it
was said to them, 'You are not My people,' there, it shall
be said to them, 'You are sons of the living God.'"

In chapter two, God describes this tough love and its
painful consequences. The people will return to God and
realize all the good He had done for them and how they
lost it all by placing the things of the world above God.
Again, the church is called the bride of Christ, and this
word pictures the wife (God's people) committing adultery against her Husband (God). Again and again God
says, "You went after (other) lovers." (Hosea 2:5,13)

But, listen to what God says of His adulterous bride.
Listen to the love for her (us). "Therefore, behold, I will
allure her, will bring her into the wilderness, and speak
comfort to her. I will give her vineyards from there. And
the valley of Achor (Trouble) as a door of hope; She shall
sing there, as in the day of her youth, as in the day when
she came up from the land of Egypt. And it shall be in that
day," says the Lord, "That you will call Me, 'my *Husband*',
and *no longer* call Me, '*my Master*'". (Hosea 2:14-16)

God goes on to promise that He will protect them from
evil and give them peace, and then, even after all they'd
done, He says... "I will betroth you to Me forever; Yes, I
will betroth you to Me in righteousness and justice, in
loving kindness and mercy; I will betroth you to Me in
faithfulness, and you shall know the Lord. It shall come
to pass in that day that I will answer," says the Lord. "I
will answer the heavens and they shall answer the earth."
(Hosea 2:19-21) God says He will provide them all they
need (22). Then, verse 23 expresses His love and desire.

"Then, I will sow her *for Myself* in the earth. And I will have mercy on her who had not obtained mercy. Then I will say to those who were not My people, 'You are My people!' And they shall say, 'You are my God!'" (Hosea 2:23)

I am yours and you are mine, says God! This is God foretelling what would be done with us when Christ came.

Look back at verses 19 and 20, "I will betroth you to Me in *righteousness* and *justice*, in *loving kindness* and *mercy*. I will betroth you to Me in *faithfulness*."

This is a picture of the cross. God brought righteousness (right standing with God) through justice and mercy in loving kindness. Together at the cross both justice (judgment of sin) and love's mercy (God's sacrifice of His Son for us) were joined. In faithfulness (our trust in this fact) we shall know the Lord as His betrothed wife.

God is faithful to us and says, "You are My people!" When we say, "You are my God!" we are joined with Him in an unbreakable covenant forever. This is God's ultimate desire. But to make His point that He is completely and honorably committed to His faithfulness, He told Hosea to go again and love a woman who is committing adultery. God was showing Hosea His heart to love His people and how that felt in light of their behavior.

Again, He laid out the consequences that would befall them each time they left Him for the love of "the world". When we forsake God and trust in wealth and pleasures of sin, we are climbing in bed with the enemy. We are committing adultery against our true Husband, the One who has betrothed (committed) Himself to us and died to save us from that enemy.

Understand, we have a choice. There is no love without free will, and we can choose evil over good, just as many young men and women choose someone who is bad for them rather than good. These choices have consequences. As exciting as it may seem to go with the rebellious person who lives fast and loose, there is unavoidable trouble which follows them. So it is, when we choose Satan's way over God's.

"The more they increased, the more they sinned against Me." (Hosea 4:7)

The more God blessed His people, the more they wanted, and the worse their behavior became. Isn't this precisely what happens when we enable someone we love to continue in their obsessions and addictions? When we continue allowing them to abuse us and those around them? It is almost an immutable characteristic within the human psyche when there are no serious consequences to our odious actions, we will inevitably perpetuate them.

God said, "There is no truth or mercy or knowledge of God in the land. By swearing and lying, killing and stealing and committing adultery, they break all restraint with bloodshed upon bloodshed." (Hosea 4:2)

God says, "You don't even acknowledge Me or goodness and you continue to hurt each other with all this evil, without holding back." (paraphrase)

Tell me, if your children are hurting each other, what do you do? Do you say, "Well, it's unloving to punish them. I'll just hope they stop on their own"? I promise you, if this is your approach (and it is for many), you will be raising some very toxic and dangerous people. In the next verse, God shows them the consequences for such behavior.

"Therefore, the land will mourn; and everyone who dwells there will waste away..." (Hosea 4:3)

Think of what would happen to this nation without any laws, without consequences for stealing, killing, or rape. We enforce limits on bad behavior, because without those limits, our nation would "waste away" into an evil anarchy. We also do this because our very nature demands justice. Even the most rebellious among us believe that wrong must be righted. So, why do we question, criticize, and even condemn God for exercising this principle? Again, we are beings of justice because we were created in His likeness.

To reiterate a point; when we choose recreation on the devil's playground, we are subject to his rules. This is from which God seeks to defend us. Like children who are oblivious to the pedophilic predator lurking in the shadows of the playgrounds edge, we rebelliously wander off on a path of our own and into the hands of evil. Like naïve children we do not comprehend the restrictive boundaries imposed by our heavenly parent are dutifully placed out of love for our protection.

Hosea 5:4 says, "They do not direct their deeds toward turning to their God. For the *spirit* of harlotry is *in their midst*. And they do not know the Lord." When we are in the middle of Satan's territory, he uses our desires to blind our eyes to God. And know this—God will allow you to see all you will find there is destruction.

If God protected you (from consequence) while you were engaged in evil, He would be condoning it and sending you a clear message that it's ok to partake of it. No, He will send you the same message you would send your child. Evil equals pain and destruction.

Proverbs 14:12 states: "There is a way which seems right to a man, but its end is the way to death." (ESV) God told Hosea, they are "oppressed and broken in judgement, because they willingly walked by human precept (human rules of thought). Therefore, I will be like a moth to him and to his house like rottenness." (Hosea 5:11-12)

> "I will return again to My place till they acknowledge their offense. Then they will seek

My face; *in their affliction* they will earnestly seek Me." (Hosea 5:15)

Then they will say, "Come and let us return to the Lord. For He has torn, but He will heal us. He has stricken, but He will bind (bandage) us up. After two days, He wills revive us. On *the third day, He will raise* us up. That we may live in His sight. Let us *know*, let us *pursue* the *knowledge* of God. His going forth is as established as the morning." (Hosea 6:1-3) God's existence and true faithfulness is as sure as the sun rising in the morning, they said. Pursue the knowledge of God and you will avoid destruction. This is what we call a "no brainer," common sense. If God knows all and sees all and His wisdom and love are complete, then why in the world would we fail to practically recognize its value? We'll address this question soon.

You see, it's not as if these people didn't know who God was, or why their lives were in ruin. They stated clearly what they knew to do. "Let us return to the Lord." And they stated clearly what they knew God would do with their return. "He will heal. He will bandage. He will revive. He will raise us up!" He was as sure as the morning dawning the next day to do this. They said, "He will come to us like rain." Rain is life. Rain is restoration and new life.

You cannot just read the *judgments* of God out of context or aside from the fact that God had delivered His people from the bondage and oppression of slavery in Egypt and had "raised" them as His own children, instructing them in His precepts and character.

The Passover was kept as an eternal memorial to the love, goodness, and power of God and extinguished all previous doubt about His intentions toward the children of Israel.

Like your children, they knew they were loved, and they also knew the rules of the household. How many of you know that the younger children look up to the older? How God dealt with the children of Israel put God's character and all truth concerning Him on display for every human who would ever be born. He wasn't just setting the example and standard for them, but for the on-looking gaze of all humanity. To fail to establish these truths would have placed all of His children in the dark danger of ignorance. "My people are destroyed from lack of knowledge." (Hosea 4:6)

I have a cousin, more so a friend, who described the Bible as a "tough read." He joked that, "The character development is a bit abrupt." Though I certainly understood his quip, I stated that the Bible is an eternal Book, about two characters, God and man, and the character development is anything but abrupt. In fact, it took millennia, and stands alone as the most patiently and powerfully detailed character development in the history of mankind. It is the story of the Creator of the universe and His interaction with His creation. If you will read it in this light, carefully considering the behaviors revealed by both characters, open your mind to what is being consistently unveiled about them, without preconceived bias or presumptuous logic, simply imagining it true at face value, it can do nothing but capture you.

Look at Hosea 6:4-6, and listen to the following declaration. See if this doesn't sound all too familiar.

"Oh Ephraim, what shall I do to you? Oh Judah, what shall I do to you? For your faithfulness is like a morning cloud, and like the early dew it goes away. Therefore, I have hewn (formed, shaped) them by the prophets; I have slain them by the words of My mouth: And your judgments are like light that goes forth. For I desire mercy not sacrifice, and knowledge of God more than burnt offerings."

Now, put your child's name in place of "Ephraim" and "Judah"-

"Oh, Eddy and Jimmy, what am I going to do with you? When will you listen and do what I've told you? Why must you disobey me every day? I tell you, and it goes in one ear and out the other. I've told you, and your mother has told you a hundred times, so there's no excuse. You're old enough to know better, and you've been shown this clearly, again and again. I don't enjoy punishing you. Do you know that? I'd much rather let you off the hook than have to ground you. I would rather you listened to what I know is best for you instead of forcing me to bring these consequences."

Do you ever find yourself praying on your way home from work that your kids didn't do something you were going to have to reprimand them for? "When I would've healed Israel, then the iniquity of Ephraim was uncovered." (Hosea 7:1)

"I just wanted to come home and have a pleasant evening, laughing with my kids, but then, "Jimmy got into trouble today; you need to deal with your son!"

Of course, the scale is a bit different, but the heart of the matter is the same. Right is right and wrong is wrong. We reward right behavior and rebuke and discipline wrong behavior for the good of our children and society. God would rather have mercy than judgment, but He will not allow the destruction that comes with unchecked rebellion.

God tells us that "destruction awaits all those who flee from Him." (Hosea 7:13) I spoke of the improbable scenario, in my last book, "The Captain's Pen," in which a parent would allow their defiant five-year-old child to run away from home. Can you imagine allowing them to walk out into the uncertain night and fend for themselves? This is the plight of our God.

A temporary fix for this rebellion would be simply to slip out another door and behind a bush and mimic a few spooky sounds for your naïve renegade and then watch him bolt back to the safety of your house to think long and hard if that thought ever crossed his mind again. Better that *you* scare him straight than to subject him to a legitimate threat of danger.

Very plainly, the big picture is that God is a Husband and Father protecting His wife and children from the evil of the world. There are physical predators from which we must protect our family. We understand that if we don't stay close to our wife and children, and in constant communication with them, they are vulnerable to the danger of predators. This dynamic is never more prevalent than at an amusement park. We keep our family together, close to us, so no one is lost.

We know that to be lost and away from our protection, they can easily and quickly become victims of evil. There is power in unity under the strength, leadership, love, and loyalty of a parent. You may or may not notice but Moms and Dads are on full alert in these situations. They are the guardian of the family, and obedience is key. The most important concern is the constant command, "Stay *close* to me!" This is the very heart of your God for *His* wife and children.

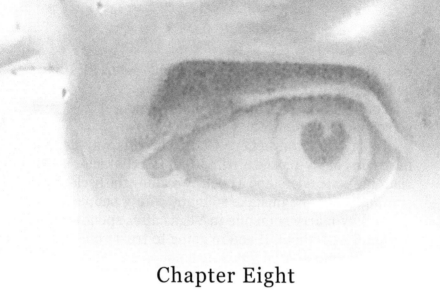

Chapter Eight
NOT MY TYPE

"I love you the more in that I believe you had liked me for my own sake and for nothing else."
~John Keats

As much as we may wish we could create the "ideal" god of our wishes, this is a futile and irrelevant exercise. God is not Who we imagine in order to justify our lifestyles or fit our world view. God is completely unaffected by our willful ignorance or self-serving rationalizations to impose our finite imaginations on Him. He is Who He is.

In fact, it is the height of self-delusion and manipulative deceit to knowingly manufacture a character opinion of someone you do not know, simply to ease your conscience. For the life of me, I cannot comprehend this absurdity of human nature to attribute characteristics to someone where no such characteristics have ever been displayed. Or worse! When those characteristics have been blatantly contradicted.

You will not worship someone you do not love, and you cannot love someone you do not know!

To say that you believe God to be this way or that based on cherry-picked attributes of His character is like claiming you understand a book by reading the back-cover summary. It's the mistake so many young people make when they marry someone in Vegas after spending the weekend with them. If you're going to trust your future, especially your eternal future, to someone, you had better know that person's character.

If knowing the true God is possible, why would you settle for a self-deceived guess concerning Him and risk so much to simply comfort a temporary rationalization to ineffectively justify your lifestyle.

People who convince themselves of a god who will affirm the standard of "right" that allows them to sleep at night are on the same level with those who've ignored multiple doctor's diagnoses of cancer until they finally found one who will tell them what they want to hear. This is called denial. Regardless of what they've chosen to believe, the authentic truth will inevitably arrive.

As many times in my life as I've wished someone were a certain way, those heartfelt wishes did nothing to change or affect who that someone truly was. And as many times as I wished I could fail to pay traffic tickets and still avoid jail, well, let's just say that wishful thinking has no effect on the sovereignty of the great state of Texas.

You've heard the saying, "You don't get to choose your parents." An equal matter of fact is that you don't get to choose your God. The truth is, we don't really want a god who would comply with all our reasoning— or one who would patronize us. We don't want a mate or spouse who would do this either.

Inherently, we understand that we are imperfect. We are quite aware of our tendencies to selfishly miss the mark, take things for granted, or engage in self-destructive behavior.

Have you ever met someone you were very attracted to but who agreed with everything you said, gave into any whim or demand, apologized every other minute, and never put there foot down to stand up for a contradicting view? This kind of person is a bore and quite frankly drives us crazy. It's very hard to grasp at the least bit of respect for this type of obsessively catering "yes man." By nature, we find ourselves purposely pushing their boundaries in hope that there are some. Why do you suppose this is? On the surface, it would seem that someone who would conform to our every desire and agree with our every notion would be exactly what we would want, but it's not.

We want someone who will check us when we are unreasonable or flat out wrong. Accordingly, we would have no respect for a god who would conform to us rather than lead us. But this is precisely what so many are doing by our impotent assumption and arrogant expectation regarding our placement of God into a convenient position that won't disrupt our lives.

We attempt to mold or fashion a god who gives an approving pat on the back for the "good stuff" we do and has a gracefully blind eye for the little "white lie." We may think this is the god we want, when if, in reality we found out He was truly like this, we'd want nothing to do with him. Why? If we knew he were okay with even one lie, we would never trust him. If we had a god who was accepting of the least of evils, we would question any profession of his goodness.

If God were able to engage in deceit or overlook injustice in one instance, we would question the whole of His integrity. When you discover someone has lied, even if not to you, there will always be doubt as to the validity of their honesty in all things.

If your spouse made light of the fact that his best friend had cheated on his wife, what thoughts might you have about the importance of their faithfulness to you? Character, human character, is a fragile thing. Good or bad behavior in one area or circumstance easily bleeds over into others.

There is a peace and security in the knowledge that the ones we are to trust are solid, unchanging, and reliably worthy of our trust. Agreement is not always necessary, but honesty and integrity are indispensable. True love is without fear. The Bible says, "There is no fear in love, but perfect love casts out fear." (1 John 4:18) Without complete trust, there is fear. Fear only enters in the absence of trust. The two cannot coexist. True trust cannot exist in the presence of fear. Without *complete* trust, there is fear. And so, without trust, there can be no authentic love.

Love defines itself by sacrifice. Love is not "butterflies" in your stomach or goosebumps on your skin. Love is an action word which can only validate itself sacrificially. Trust is the essence of love and can only be ultimately gained through sacrifice.

Love is not proved genuine by speech absent a corroborative action of commitment. Honesty in one's character is the springboard from which that action is executed. A person's motives are as important as their actions. If we see God as a person who compromises any part of His character, we will subsequently question the credibility of His actions, causing us insecurity, doubt, and fear.

God has established again and again the demonstrative fact that *He does not change.*

Because His promises do not change concerning evil, sin, and their unavoidable consequence, our confidence is established in His promises concerning good toward us.

If your type of "god" compromises to overlook injustice or wrongdoing, he could be rightly questioned as to whether he would compromise his commitment in respect to faithfully delivering on his good promises.

You *want* a God who always does what He says, every time.

You *want* a God of mercy, and you *want* a God of justice.

His implementation of either cannot be allowed to disqualify the other in even one instance, or else neither would hold any genuine value. Only a God who is able to balance these two imperatives perfectly could be considered good and worthy of worship. No Character who fails to hold evil accountable can be considered righteously good. And no Character who lacks mercy and the willingness to sacrifice can be considered lovingly good. Any god who would contradict himself in any way or at any turn regarding these essential principles would be disqualified from the definition of good and can never be confidently and empirically validated or confirmed as perfectly *good*. We must understand that we are not qualified to recognize perfection as it relates to good. We can but aspire to imagine its complete reality.

Even where it has been displayed for us, the true nature of goodness escapes us. For millennia, theologians have sought to explain how both mercy and judgment were completely fulfilled in the cross of Christ. And many have tragically reasoned themselves in and then right out of its truth.

Convincing themselves that because they cannot wrap a finite mind around the infinite wisdom of God, the reason is somehow flawed or fallible. Instead of recognizing the obvious benefit this conundrum reveals, that God is greater, reason becomes the "reason" for their fall from grace. My Husky, Max, has faith in me. He doesn't comprehend the why. He simply understands that I am greater.

> "God is not a man that He should lie, not a human being, that He should change His mind. Does He speak and then not act? Does He promise and not fulfill?" (Numbers 23:19)

By consciously conforming God's character to ours in order to dispel guilt, we regulate God to an ineffective position in our life which holds no more power or ability than we do. It's no wonder that we then lack any confidence or true faith in Him. All we've managed to do is temporarily subvert what our hearts know to be true. To avert a sense of guilt we desperately hope will not return.

The problem is, when we fall into the canyon, we thought was a rut, subconsciously, our mind now holds the image of a god who was not critically engaged with integrity while the "good times" were rolling, so we lack the faith to now see him as constructively engaged with the same integrity in our rescue. You see, we think we want it both ways. We think we want "the god of grace" while we're engaged in sin who will compromise the execution of his word concerning sin. We then wish Him to switch characters when we are facing the consequence of that sin, to keep his word to deliver us.

However, we cannot and should not have confident faith in that god. It is a contradiction to all reason. If God knows sin will destroy us, and then rewards us for taking part in it, we would not only submerse ourselves in destruction but then consider ourselves justified in blaming Him for it. It flies directly in the face of integrity to be consistent with respect to some things and fluid or unsteady in respect to others.

It is not that God cannot or will not deliver us. It is that our faith has no power to see God as bigger than our problem after convincing ourselves that He was uninvolved with or apathetic to the cause of those problems to begin with.

If we do not see God's immutable conviction and commitment to oppose sin, we will not see Him as unwavering and faithful in His equally unshakeable love for us. We carry these imaginations about God because we don't know Him. Without the authentic knowledge of truth concerning Him we are simply forced to imagine what He may be like. We fail to see Him as He truly is. This is particularly unfortunate and unnecessary when it comes to those who have received Him as their Savior.

So many who were called by the Spirit of truth to believe Jesus died for them don't grasp the fact that He did so to have a relationship with them which continues to grow. It's exactly like getting married to someone and never speaking to them again. You met, fell in love, moved in together, but then you moved into a room at the other end of the house and have ignored your spouse ever since. How heartbroken might you be if this happened to you?

The Bible says that we inherit resurrection life, eternal life through Christ. So many of us simply married Christ for His inheritance. We have gotten what we wanted out of the relationship—life eternal, fire insurance. This Man paid the ultimate price for us. When we were destined for hell, He stepped in for His bride and stood up for her. He said whatever it takes to see her safe always and forever, I will do it. Whatever it takes to save her from a torturous eternity, I will do it. When this truth actually dawns on you, you will truly fall in love. You will move as close to Him as you can get. And you will want to know Him personally instead of imagining who He is or what He is like. Until then, we choose to imagine we can take what we

want from Him and leave the unknown, and the poten-
tially inconvenient, right where it is.

We choose to imagine that because God is love (and
He is), He overlooks or condones wrong behavior, as if to
say, "Well, boys will be boys!" or humans will be human.
We choose to see Him saying, "This *little* sin isn't a big
deal," when it's convenient for us. "After all, we are forgiven because of Jesus, right? We aren't saved by works
anyway. It's by grace... He made me, so, He understands."

What I want you to see is that you are missing the
beauty and power of what you possess in intimate relationship with Him. When you finally catch that He is head-
over-heals in love with you, when the magnitude of that
love and commitment dawns on you, you will no longer
abstain from sin just because it's wrong. Once you fully
grasp the depths of His unchangeable love for you, you
will fall in love with Him. From then on, that love is what
will drive you to want to honor Him, and nothing else.

Remember, on that day, "you will no longer call Me
Master, but you will call Me Husband.... I will betroth you
to Me forever; I will betroth you in righteousness and justice, in love and compassion." (Hosea 2:16, 19)

What most won't see is, if we were able to construct a
god from our imagination, his wisdom and power would
extend no further than the borders of ours. In light of
what we perceive as great progress socially, the impact,
however well-intentioned, through the wisdom of mankind over the ages of history, has failed to produce any
meaningful and universally growing integrity—much less
a truly selfless love.

In fact, the accumulated waters of man's wisdom seem
to continually evaporate in the fires of narcissism rather
than extinguish it. It's been said with simple elegance and
glaring truth that, "The heart of the human problem is the
problem of the human heart." (Adrian Rogers)

If people were honest and you could pull back the curtain on the general motives of people who act "selflessly," you would see but two. It's either to ease their own guilt, or to place them in a favorable light in the eyes of others to achieve an agenda which ultimately serves them. True self-sacrifice for no other reason but to meet needs for that person's exclusive joy is very rare. Non-existent? No, but rare. I suggest sacrifice in pure and genuine sincerity is the exception to the overwhelming cause to serve one's self.

There's a reason this is true. Once man's eyes were open to both good and evil, simultaneously the Spirit of God (the source of good) was dispelled by evil, as they cannot coexist. Man was separated indefinitely from the only source of true good he had. His nature was changed in an instant, because as he became separated from the source of true good, true wisdom left with it. He was not only disconnected from the Spirit of selfless love but from truth all together. From that day forward, man's truth would be unavoidably filtered through the innate craving to serve himself. Mankind is perpetually handicapped from true wisdom by the blinding glare of the darkness of self. His greatest obstacle in pursuit of truth is the inescapable deceit of his own heart.

"The heart is deceitful above all things and *beyond cure*. Who can understand it?" (Jeremiah 17:9)

We have been separated, cut off like a branch from a tree, or like a tree uprooted and placed in the desert. Jeremiah tells us that when we are connected to the Spirit of God we are, "like a tree planted by the water that sends out its roots by the stream. It does not fear when heat comes; its leaves are always green. It has no

worries in a year of drought and never fails to bear fruit."
(Jeremiah 17:8)

The word of God will always confirm itself, reaffirming
one truth with another. In John 15, Jesus establishes the
truth He had given Jeremiah ages before.

> "I am the Vine; you are the branches. If you
> remain in Me and I in you, you will *bear* much
> *fruit;* apart from Me you can do nothing. If you
> do not remain in Me, you are like a branch that
> is thrown away and withers; such branches are
> picked up, thrown in the fire and burned. If you
> remain in Me and My words remain in you, ask
> whatever you wish, and it will be done for you.
> This is to My Father's glory, that you bear much
> fruit, showing yourselves to be My disciples. As
> the Father has loved Me, so have I loved you.
> Now remain in My love." (John 15:5-9)

So, when a person says that the God of the Bible is not
Someone they understand, or relate to, or that they have
a hard time believing in this God, this is exactly the only
response that would make sense to the natural mind.

Without the Spirit of God to pull back the curtain, or
remove our blinders, or set aside our self-tainted glasses
to receive true wisdom and understanding, we are unable
to relate. The very fact that we are separated from this
ability to reach beyond our comprehension or admit that
there is any truth beyond the borders of ourselves, only
serves the point and exposes our greatest problem. God
is not our "type!" Much more importantly, without our
way back to Him, our connection to Him, namely Jesus,
we are not *His* "type."

"For what do light and darkness have to do with one another?" 2 (Corinthians 6:14)

"There is a way that seems right to a man, but its end is the way of death." (Proverbs 14:12)

Notice, it says "there is a way that *seems*" (or appears) to be right. This verse assumes that man is inclined to rely on his own wisdom and believe it to be right, but in fact, it will only serve to lead him to death.

People ask, "What does one man's death on a Roman cross two-thousand years ago have to do with me?" To pull this event out of the text and attempt to find some application to us without the knowledge that the entirety of God's Word provides us might indeed seem foolish at face value.

"For the message of the cross is foolishness to those who are perishing, but to us who are being saved, it is the power of God." (1 Corinthians 1:18)

To think our inability to fully grasp something must mean it's not true is counter even to man's own logic. If science has taught us anything, it is assumptions make fools of anyone who chooses to make them.

For it is written, "I will destroy the wisdom of the wise; the intelligence of the intelligent, I will frustrate. Where is the wise person? Where is the teacher of the law? Where is the philosopher of this age? Has not God made foolish the wisdom of the world?" (1 Corinthians 1:19-20)

On a regular basis within the scientific community, theories are debunked, proclamations of discovery are undone, what was thought to be ironclad dissolves, and even what was accepted enough to teach our children in grade school comes crumbling down.

The wisdom of the wise is destroyed, the intelligence of the intelligent is frustrated, and the "wisdom" of the world is realized as foolish. Science, the knowledge of man, is a constantly reproving process of blunders. It is an exercise in humility which has taken us from a flat earth, to our solar system being the limit of the universe, from an eternal universe which was stagnant, to a big bang from "nothing," from a steadily expanding universe, to an accelerating universe, from a moon made of cheese, to watching a man step onto its surface. New and exciting discoveries have taken us from "dark matter," (invisible something) and "dark energy," (invisible power) to a large community of scientists open to the possibility of creation having an intelligent designer. The arrogance of man in light of every embarrassing misstep is unaccountable.

What baffles my mind is even from a human perspective, man's wisdom is blatantly presented as foolishness. He has chosen to place his faith in all his collective analysis, in the unprovable, un-evidenced and obviously blundered theory of evolution, as an explanation, as a serious and sincere explanation of his existence. Stating just as sincerely this all began with some cosmic explosion, which he is unable to deny came from absolutely nothing and with no cause. As I've stated, with all the evidence, it takes more faith to believe in this foolishness than in a Creator God. With all to the contrary, the atheist defiantly insists on the reality of this imagination.

Make no mistake, this worldview is more a religion than science. For obvious reasons, it places man as the master of his destiny, in control of his circumstances, and most importantly, unaccountable to anything or anyone above him. He is the king of his world and therefore "free" from the belief that he may be in need of anything. By this he proclaims that the created can know its purpose without consulting the Creator.

Assuming this belief, with all he knows about the fallibility of human wisdom, he has put himself in the place of God. What he fails to see, what his pride has blinded him to, is by assuming control of his destiny, he has also assumed the responsibility for his own soul. He will have nothing more than his own power and his own resources when the truth is revealed.

When he is called forward and asked whose name is on his ticket and what God is in his heart, he will be forced to say "mine." When asked by whose power and wisdom he intends to enter heaven, he will be forced to say "mine." When the light begins to fade, he will know that pride was not the price for admission to heaven but to that other place. And as the next in line is questioned, he will hear the response his heart had rejected time and time again, "HIS."

> "For since in the wisdom of God the world, *through its wisdom did not know Him,* God was pleased through the foolishness of what was preached to save those who believe." (1 Corinthians 1:21) "But to those called by God to salvation... Christ is the power of God and the wisdom of God." "For the foolishness of God is wiser than human wisdom and the weakness of God is stronger than human strength." (1 Corinthians 1:24-25) "But God chose the foolish things of the world to shame the wise; God chose the weak things of the world to shame the strong." (1 Corinthians 1:27)

Man was created in His image and began as His "type." But Adam fell from grace and his spirit could no longer reside with God. God had lost His bride. So, He came—in His Son—to be human and make us His "type" again.

The fact that we naturally reject this premise exposes its validity.

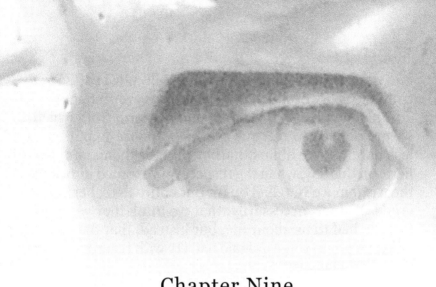

Chapter Nine

DIVIDED DEVOTIONS

"The young always have the same problem—how to rebel and conform at the same time. They have now solved this by defying their parents and copying one another." ~Quentin Crisp

I remember the contrast of emotions I held as a teenager. One half of me was battling the insecurities of puberty and corporate acceptance. The other half was excited about every new discovery in a world much different than what had previously been presented to me. I distinctively recall a sense of invincibility and an idealistic view of the opportunities unfolding in front of me.

There is a point in most of our lives when we slip the bonds of our parents' reasoning to embrace ideas, however abstract, which we believe our parents, and indeed the world, have somehow missed. We can't always put it into words, but it is as if we have magically grasped a secret truth or reality of which no one else has ever thought.

This "epiphany" is the root and platform from which we are obliged to roll our eyes in response to our clueless parents. We almost harbor pity for them, and it is here, on this day, when the respect we've leaned into, and the wisdom we've relied on for our entire lives, begins to erode. It's not, necessarily, that we think they've intentionally lied to us about life, but instead, that they have fallen victim to some archaic naivety with regard to what the world really is.

Suddenly, our fifteen-year-old mind has decided that our well-meaning parents have been duped and have missed it for four or five decades. After all, they didn't even have smart phones, internet, or Uber when they were growing up. As dad has repeatedly stated, he had no more than a bicycle and a stick to entertain himself! How could anyone have true wisdom about life when they have a hard time surfing the net or using a GPS device.

We mistakenly assume since it is painfully obvious we have more "knowledge" than our parents concerning the beneficial tools of the day, we must possess more wisdom. How could they possibly relate or offer any relevant direction for a world they have never lived in and are just trying to keep up with?

This has always been the "rub," if you will, from one generation to the next. However, this logic has gained a much more credible momentum in the young mind of the twenty first century—where virtually anything they want to know is a click or a touch away.

Though technology, fashion, access to information, and approach to social issues inevitably change, human nature does not. Character, both good and evil, is inescapably timeless. Certain traits of the human condition are unaffected by modern implementations and do not evolve over any amount of time or influence.

This is not to say that a corporate civility cannot be adopted or improved, and moral rules enforced. We know this is accomplished historically. Even so, realizing there should be civilized parameters and even a progressive system to regulate it, has no affect to change the intrinsic nature of the human psyche. In fact, the very purpose of judicial integrity is there, by necessity, to discourage and press back the innate compulsion of man to give in to his *natural* temptations. Without the timeless force of the human's inclination to evil, no such system would be required.

My point is this—the most basic and important issues requiring wisdom, the nature of man's relation to himself and others, has not and never will change.

Here is what I hope young and invincible spirits will honestly open your minds to consider. Both good and evil reside, respectfully, within humans. Not just among us as an idea, but within us and around us as literal forces. Much like light and darkness, they oppose and affect each other. Our devotion, loyalty, and engagement with respect to either will perpetuate their presence, influence, and tangible ramifications in our lives and those with whom we interact. In the natural, light overpowers darkness instantly. Bring in light, and darkness is dispelled. The more light there is the less darkness can remain. Now, see this, the amount of darkness we experience in our lives is determined by the amount of light with which we are devoted to surrounding ourselves.

Just as is true in the natural, so goes the supernatural world, or if you like, the spiritual world. Just as the sun was provided to light the world, and men have harnessed that energy to power artificial light, God's glory and power is what lights the spirit realm. Darkness has no more power in the spiritual realm to overcome this light than it has in the natural.

Since Jesus created all things, the Bible states that He is life, and that life is the light of mankind.

> "Through Him all things were made; without Him nothing was made that has been made. In Him was life, and that life was the *light of all mankind*. The light shines in the darkness, and *the darkness has not overcome it*." (John 1:3-5)

In the spirit of men and in the dimension of heaven, goodness, or Holiness (absence or separation from evil), is light, and shines out of the glory of God. And evil (the opposite or absence of good) is darkness and is a result of our fallen nature as separated from God by the disobedience of Adam and our inherited nature to *willingly* embrace that disobedience.

Without our *willingness* to allow Christ to shine His light into our life, we are absent that light, and absence of light leaves darkness. Even as Christians who have received the gift of salvation from Christ's sacrifice at the cross, we can still walk in darkness while we are unwilling to allow His light to shine into every corner of our lives.

As I have shared, Jesus didn't face down the horror and agony of the cross simply to buy your way into heaven one day. He said that He "came so that you may have *life* and have it more abundantly!" What did we read was life? Life is the light of all mankind. We seem to want all the pros and to have nothing to do with the cons. Before His promise of abundant life in John 10:10- Jesus tells us that the thief (Satan) comes to steal, kill, and destroy!"

Where there is no light from Jesus there is darkness. There is no neutral ground. There is no place between light and darkness. Remember Jesus said, "you are either for Me or against Me." This is not because of some ego trip and it's not about control. This is about protecting you out of love. We are like a soldier lost and alone on the battlefield surrounded by enemies when suddenly a special ops elite commando shows up to rescue us. He shouts "We're going to get you out of here! Follow me!" When we reject Christ, we say "no thanks, I'll find my way...I can make it."

"Are you crazy, kid!? The chopper's waiting and I'm all you've got son!"

Tragically, this soldier, and countless others like him, are taken into a torturous captivity and die in the darkness of their own pride.

They've chosen to believe the lie that they are smarter and stronger than the Captain who seeks to save them.

When we choose to divide our devotions between good and evil, light and darkness, we will inevitably begin to prefer darkness. Why? Because the light we do have is just enough to expose the dark places for what they truly are rather than how we've chosen to see them. Have you ever laid in the dark and seen an object and imagined it as something different from what it was? This is an easy exercise in the dark, but when the room is fully lit, you are forced to see things as they actually are.

The more we choose the dark, the more accustomed to it we become. The longer your eyes are in darkness, the more they adapt to it until soon it becomes "normal," natural in a sense. No one can fully see you and you are not forced to see what ugliness surrounds you. This is why people stay in the dark. A little light comes in from time to time, but when it shines on something we're ashamed of, we close that door.

The problem with this is as other things creep in around us, we're unable to see the danger they present. We walk through the dilapidated house of a dark life bumping into dangerous things and overlooking the ways out until the floor gives way and we find ourselves trapped in an even darker basement. Our eyes can no longer adapt to this blackness, and we start to think we will never escape it.

Two days ago, my wife arrived at work to learn of a horrifying tragedy. The beautiful, young daughter of her good friend and co-worker had taken her own life. The victim of a self-inflicted gunshot wound to her head, the Austin sheriff had discouraged the mother's instinct to fly down, stating, "This is not something you want to see ma'am."

As I've previously revealed, I've been there. Not in this mother's place, thank God, but in that hopelessly dark place which offers no way out. Light becomes so extremely foreign that you have forgotten not just what good looks like, but even the very concept. Good simply seems to mean the absence of bad; take away the bad and there will be good. I'm bad. Remove me and good will enter.

But bad can only be removed by good. Not your good, His.

Darkness can only be removed by light. Not your light, His.

When the young buy into the lie that they have more wisdom than their parents, when we buy the lie that we are wiser than God, we become open to outside influence.

"They have rejected the good; the enemy will pursue them." (Hosea 8:3)

God says, "When you reject the light, there will only be darkness. When you reject My way, you open the door to evil."

It's natural to want to be your own person, and Satan uses this to convince you that those who love you only seek to control you. God has created only *one* you and your individuality is on purpose and for purpose. No one's asking you to become someone else. In fact, He has not created you to fit in, but to stand out!

You will have an influence for good that no one else in all of history could accomplish.

It's true—you are not your parents. You know things and possess certain powers and insight no other person has ever had combined in quite the same way as you. So, when you observe the fact you are unique in respect to your parents, understand that it doesn't mean that you must be opposed to them. Instead, realize your abilities have been provided to supplement what was lacking in your team.

> 1 Corinthians 12:21-25 says it so well: "The eye cannot say to the hand, 'I don't need you!' On the contrary, those parts of the body that seem to be weaker are indispensable... -But God has put the body together, giving greater honor to the parts that lacked it, so that there should be no division in the body, but that its parts should have equal concern for each other."

When we honor our parents with the understanding they are weaker in some areas and honorably strong in others, we see there is strength in unity. A mutual family structure of love supports each other. Indeed, it completes each other.

Verse 26 and 27 which follow the above expresses the beneficial results of this maturity. "If one part suffers, every part suffers with it; if one part is honored, every part rejoices with it. You are the body of Christ and each one of you is a part of it."

This unity is precisely what our enemy seeks to divide. Again, war strategy 101 is to divide and conquer. It's scary how quickly and easily the rebellious nature, which causes us to declare our independence from our parents, is used to attach us in allegiance to a person we barely know and to serve an ancient agenda.

If the "family" I've been describing is foreign to your experience and something you've never really known, then consider these amazing promises...

"God is a Father to the fatherless... and sets the lonely in families." (Psalm 68:5-6)

"... -to look after orphans and widows in their distress and to keep oneself from being polluted by the world." (James 1:27)

"The Lord watches over the foreigner and sustains the fatherless and the widow but He frustrates the ways of the wicked" (Psalm 146:9)

Or- "because I (God) rescue the poor who cried for help, and the fatherless who had none to assist them." (Job 29:12)

The Bible says, "...the rebellious will live in a sun-scorched land." (Psalm 68:6)

"My people are destroyed for lack of knowledge." (Hosea 4:6)

Wherever you may find yourself today, the past does not have to equal the future. And whether you know it or not, there is a loving Father who pursues you and wants so desperately for you to join His eternal family. Jesus said, "All people will know you by your love for one another." (John 13:35)

If rebellion has left you empty or in despair, if you find yourself without family, call on your heavenly Father and find His children. I know it may make no real sense to you at all, but perhaps He knew that this dire circumstance would be the only way He could save you. And if you do have family, consider the ones who do not, and don't take one more hour for granted. Do what you must to be reconciled with them.

Two armies are being built. Two kingdoms are being filled. Two ways are being chosen. Two truths are being presented. One by love. One by selfish rebellion, more commonly known as pride.

There are only two groups of people. One group is boarding a ship and trusting a Captain to bring them to a distant shore. Another group is determined to swim the depths of a vast ocean themselves.

We all must cross this ocean, and we will not all make it.

Love says, "The distance is too great, come with Me." Pride says, "It doesn't seem that far to me. I'll take my chances."

Only *one* is right. Only *you* can choose. The provision of Love's life ~or~ The peril of pride's perdition.

Your parents and ancestors have been dealing with the issues of life, the circumstances of adversity, and the nature of people a long time before you were even a thought. A quick glance or shallow study of history will expel every confidence in regard to any notion that humanity has experienced drastic or even moderate change over time.

If you were to travel back in time for millennia, you would discover that emotions and behavior were the same then as now. Humans have, and always will, reflect certain character attributes and a lack of control over them. Love, hate, anger, joy; sadness, envy, jealousy, resentment, compassion, sacrifice, bitterness, selfishness, malice, deceit, perversion, lust, greed and gluttony;

generosity, shame, pride, jealousy and murderous rage; wickedness, carelessness, sympathy, anxiety, fear. All forms of evil and all expressions of good.

You may have very little in common with the generations that came before you concerning how you communicate over distance, how you travel, or how you entertain yourself. Your "toys" may be different as well as your access to knowledge. Your clothing may differ greatly from theirs, and you may not agree with what's cool, boss, tough, phat, wack, sick or dope.

The one thing you *will* have in common, the one thing that is universally and timelessly true for every earthling is you will inevitably and consistently be forced to interact with humans.

If you plan to stick around for any real time at all, you will also be forced to consider your health and that pesky little annoyance they call money. Social interaction, health, and money—one cannot live life and escape any of these three essentials. They are key to survival on this planet.

Incidentally, I find it interesting that in a world so bent toward the *surety of relative truth* (a contradiction to this ideology itself), no one denies their need of these things or their belief in the absolute objective truth in them.

Whatever your world view, political affiliation, gender, race, or religion, these realities, their codes for conduct or regulated norms and parameters, cannot be ignored.

This is where the adolescent mind tends to get into trouble you see. Their arrogance obtained through the things they do know better than their parents allow them to rationalize their ability to be confident in that which they don't know. Subsequently, they throw the baby out with the bath water and roll their eyes over the priceless life experience of their otherwise "clueless" parents.

My point should be obvious. Just because there are unfavorable ideas with respect to our parents, does not negate the wise and favorable directions they offer us in timeless matters. Just as important as simple lessons: "Don't play in the street. Eat your vegetables. Take a shower. Don't talk to strangers!" There are ageless relational and societal lessons covering a myriad of circumstances involved in "adulting." I ask you, how responsible would you consider a parent who denied his or her child the benefit of their wisdom and experience?

As we age and mature and have our own children, we quickly realize the error of our immaturity and how rebellion led us to discard the invaluable wisdom of those who came before us, especially those who honestly and always had our best interests in mind.

Usually, we wear some very significant scars as a result of this rebellious folly. And so, because of the damage that lies in the wake of our stubborn choices, we seek to protect our own children from making the same mistake. Then to faintly hear our former selves as our defiant thirteen-year-old whispers under his breath, *"What do you know?"* as the irony grows ever louder, the cycle repeats.

Make no mistake, prideful rebellion is intrinsic to the human mind whether it is toward an earthly or heavenly Father, and our enemy was the first to practice it. Therefore, he is quite skilled in its cultivation and promotion with respect to us. It is his sharpest tool.

What we believe about our parents and God will determine our reality. If we ignore the limits of our wisdom, ultimately our wisdom will be found in our limits. Hopefully, we survive those limits. But the truth is, sometimes we do not.

> "The wise know too well their weakness to assume infallibility: and he who knows most knows best how little he knows." ~ Thomas Jefferson

Chapter Ten

YOUR WILL BE DONE

~~~

"Fallen man is not simply an imperfect creature who needs improvement; he is a rebel who must lay down his arms." ~C.S. Lewis

In this chapter, I hope to lead you to a place outside the scope of natural borders which you may be wondering about or are already searching for. Though it might seem to be too simple, too good to be true, the answers, the formula of the truth of our existence, come down to two things: Grace and choice. We'll talk more about choice shortly.

My hope is that through the final pages of this book, you and I can try to understand, or at least plant a seed and begin a journey to understand, the most wonderful principle of God's splendid character—Grace.

We've all experienced grace in practical and natural ways. We are stopped by the policeman for speeding and though he has every right to give us a ticket, and the law requires he do so, he lets us off with a warning. We deserve a penalty for breaking the law. But, instead, the tense anxiety of fear is relieved in a moment when the officer chooses (or wills) to give us grace and another chance. He has been given authority to impose his will to override the law requirement in this circumstance, and when he does so, it's called grace.

Often, rather than sentencing an inmate to more time in jail, a judge may choose (will) to give him, or her, time served in hopes that the offender will learn from their mistake and turn their life around. By law, the judge could choose to exact the deserved punishment for the crime but in mercy and hope, he *chooses* to give grace to the offender.

Why aren't we, as a society, robotically consistent in regard to strict adherence to the penalties instituted for breaking the law? The answer is that it is imbedded in our nature as humans to forgive, to have mercy. Why is this?

Because we all recognize our tendency toward, indeed our inability to escape, mistakes. In truth, you cannot rightly define "humanity" without the element of imperfection. But it's more than our relative experience which persistently summons us to compassion. It is part of our make-up as created beings to reflect the attributes of a Creator who has made us in His likeness, or like Him.

Human grace is a by-product, a trait that we have inherited from our heavenly Father, not unlike the brown eyes or temperament you might have inherited from your earthly father.

There is a part of us which demands justice for evil. There is an equal force within us which cries for, and seeks to give, mercy. We are often fallible in our implementation or balance of these two polar forces. Our Creator, however, is perfect to this end.

He has equally as much immutable conviction to execute judgment of evil as He has unbreakable commitment and resolve to show mercy. This is what makes Him completely and perfectly good. Justice is *good*. Mercy is *good*. So, the perfect balance of these is an unquestioned, ultimate good.

As previously discussed, to fail to resolutely hold true to either of these attributes, fully and eternally, would disqualify God as perfect or good. The ability to completely fulfill His commitment to love *and* the ability to completely fulfill His commitment to rightly execute judgment of sin is what makes Him God.

We feebly attempt to accomplish this as humans, and we will only know the extent of our failure to do so somewhere in the world to come. Divergently, we will only know God's true and consummate purpose on that same great day.

However, there is one place, one event, where we are able to witness this impeccable symmetry quite clearly. It's a place called Calvary: an event known as the cross of Christ.

God's righteous judgment of man's sinful rebellion could not go unsatisfied.

At the same time, and with equal magnitude, the force of the distinction of God's enduring and indelible love was invincible. Both of these passionate instruments of unstoppable power had been racing forward, neck and neck, through eternity's portal, coequally bound in resilient destiny and relentless pursuit of the same epic point in history.

Since time began, and throughout the existence of God's people, these two magnificent forces of truth are woven in and out, again and again in a brilliant display of majestic equilibrium. God's righteous judgment was never without His loving and merciful grace.

What would seem an insurmountable paradox, what appeared an irreconcilable dilemma to our finite wisdom, had been resolved, implemented, and completed in the infinite mind of the Creator before time and space were formed. Every scenario was played out; every variable considered and then reconciled toward the ultimate fulfillment of these two unyielding forces of the character of God to pass outside the gates, climb Golgotha's hill, and collide in unison at the cross.

God's love for us, and His judgment and victory over sin, were both fulfilled in Jesus. We deserved the penalty, and that penalty was death. So, because of His love, He took the full measure of every man's deserved penalty on Himself.

Judgment fully executed. Love fully expressed.

"Therefore, there is now no condemnation for those who are in Christ Jesus, because through Christ Jesus the law of the Spirit who gives life (love) has set you free from the law of sin and death. (judgment)" (Romans 8:1-2)

"When you were dead in your sins (under judgement) ... God made you alive with Christ. He forgave us all our sins, having cancelled the charge of our legal indebtedness, which stood against us and condemned us; He has taken it away, nailing it to the cross." (Colossians 2:13-14)

If we're honest, as much as we harbor an inveterate desire to see justice done in society and the world, we don't really want justice as it relates to our own accountability to God.

To receive justice from God would mean eternal separation from Him, alone in utter darkness forever. I know people who think they'd be ok with that (or so they say). Some people even claim that's how they want it. Their own imaginative perception of God is such that they openly proclaim they want nothing to do with a God who would allow the kind of pain and suffering we find in the world.

What they fail to consider is pain and suffering are the result of man's own choice. A choice which could only be made from the act of free will. Free will was afforded us out of love to give us the greatest existence, the only authentic existence, a genuine existence, which allowed us to choose who we love, including *God*. The only reason people are able to reject God is because His love has given them free will to do so.

Understand, no one will be forced to be with God if they choose not to. And no one will have to live without God if they truly want to be with Him. God sends no one to hell. If someone goes to hell, it will be because they rejected heaven by choosing to reject the only Way to get there. This is as fair as it gets! You will get the existence in eternity that *you* choose.

God says, again and again, what His greatest desire is, "So you will be My people and I will be your God." (Jeremiah 30:22)

The key word here is *will*. "For God's *will* is that *none* should perish but that *all* would come to repentance." (2 Peter 3:9)

He *wills* (chooses) to be our God. And those who will (choose) to be His people, *will be*! Your soul is made up of your mind, will, and emotions, sometimes referred to as the heart. Remember, the Bible says that "God has placed eternity in the human heart." Whether or not you are aware, you have a longing to be close to the eternal God. God will draw us to Himself as He pursues us. Our will is the part of our soul which takes action. We can know about God, feel His tug, and become overwhelmed by emotion, but until we will or choose by action to receive Him, we are separated from Him.

Listen to (Jeremiah 30:11) and what God has chosen to do concerning you. 'I am with you and will (I choose to) save you,' declares the Lord. The same verse says, "I will discipline you but only in due measure; I will not let you go entirely unpunished."

We don't like that, but neither does my eleven-year-old. For his good, I discipline him. But, listen to the mercy behind His choice. "I will not let you go *entirely* unpunished." "Only in *due* (fair) measure." Our God is fair.

Grace is not just holding back what you deserve in penalty. It is, just as much, giving you that which you need for correction. How many times have you heard from your parents or said to your child, "I do this (punish you) because I love you."

One minute, we say, "I'd do anything for you. I'll always take up for you and protect you. I'm always on your side." And the next minute we must discipline them. Do you remember how strange this seemed when you were a child? Do you remember the moment it all became clear?

Listen to the Lord as He continues. "But all who devour you will be devoured. All your enemies will go into exile. Those who plunder you will be plundered; all who make spoil of you, I will despoil." Jeremiah 30:16 God says, "I got your back! I'm on your side. Anyone against you is against Me!" Let's continue.

Vs.17 "But, I will restore you to health and heal your wounds.' declares the Lord." ... 19~ "There will be joy and songs of thanksgiving and I will multiply My people, not diminish them; I will honor them, not despise them."

I believe Jeremiah 30:21 speaks prophetically of Jesus who will lead us and then, at the end of this verse, God asks a question. This is what I want you to see. "Their leader will be one of their own; their ruler will arise from among them. I will bring him near, and he will come close to Me." "*For who will devote himself to be close to Me?*" declares the Lord. Remember His earlier proclamation: "*So you will be My people and I will be your God.*"

God asks the question: "Who chooses to be close to Me? *That* person (the one who chooses Me) will be My person and I will be his God."

Let me ask you a question. If you were God, would you want someone to spend eternity with you who would not choose to be there with you!?

Even so, He wants them, just the same. Yes! Even the one who curses and mocks and laughs at the very notion of Him. He seeks to save. But the fair truth is this—He will not force anyone to choose Him. Again, forced love is not love at all.

His grace has saved us. His sacrifice has justified us. His love has made a way for us.

The people of Noah's day laughed and mocked and chose not to go through the door of the ark to be saved and were not forced to. Those who mock Jesus as their only way to be saved will not be forced through the Door either.

Jesus said, "I am the Door; whoever enters by Me will be saved." (John 10:9)

> *That there is only one way is not the surprise. What should amaze us is that there is any way at all!*

In light of the human standard of "goodness" and "morality" and all that is lacking in the reflection of our collective efforts, I am disgusted, and hysterically called to a sad and jaded form of laughter, at the hypocritical arrogance on display for some to imply, and even insist, that we can know and boldly proclaim what should be just or fair or right. And to have it said that God, if He is real, somehow fails to measure up.

These are those who place themselves in a fool's authority as possessing the knowledge and power in conceited pride to control their life's destiny with no regard or awareness of their limits. The smartest man on the planet holds less than one percent of all the knowledge known to mankind in all of our existence here. But, with paramount pomposity, they presume in the more than 99% of the knowledge they *do not* have, there could be no possibility that they could be wrong concerning God.

Why, then, do you suppose, as they mock, scoff, and reject Him, a fair and just God would give them anything other than what they insist they want?

Consider this: The argument they present, that God cannot be good and fair to send people to hell, implies the complaint that He will do something other than what they wish Him to do. He will not do that. He will, in fairness, allow them to have the eternity they choose to have. It would, in fact, by their own reason, be unfair to force them to be in a place with a God they do not respect, do not honor, and do not see as fair.

The strategy of our enemy is to convince you your behavior somehow excludes you. When, in truth, God came to save you *because* of the condition which causes your behavior.

The problem atheists have with God is He does not fit into the box which their condition of imperfection has built. They do not see themselves as imperfect which is congruent with the perspective an imperfect being would have. The designed is assuming the designer is in error. The mechanism is attempting to instruct the engineer as to its purpose and expectations. The created thing seems to think he knows better his purpose and limits than the Creator. While the engineer and builder of the android tries desperately to convince his creation to lie down and allow him to fix the malfunction, the android insists nothing is wrong with him.

Knowing our imperfections and consistent inconsistencies, this really should not be an idea that is difficult to fathom. And if it is such, well, then, my point is even more evident.

Let's visit a verse again to remember the honest reason this concept is rejected.

> "This is the verdict: Light has come into the world, but people loved darkness instead of light because their deeds were evil. Everyone who does evil hates the light and *will* not (choose to) come into the light for fear that their deeds will be exposed." (John 3:19-20)

People do what they want, or will, to do. In our defective souls, we don't like the light that the goodness of God shines on our imperfection, and so, we hide. We think if we even entertain the thought of coming to God, we will feel bad about certain things we do. Then we won't be able to "have fun" anymore.

The truth is that there is a reason we want to hide these things. God has made it so we know, in our conscience, they are wrong. He also knows they will rob us of all He has for us and ultimately destroy us. He wants to take us out of the darkness and into His light. Here's the coolest thing: He wants, *wills*, chooses to, place the power that raised Jesus from the dead inside of us! And let me tell you, when *that* happens, you will no longer want anything to do with the things of darkness.

While we hide, He seeks. He seeks us in our darkness.

> "For You Lord, are good, and ready to forgive, and abundant in mercy to all those who call upon You." (Psalm 86:5)

> "And all these blessings will come upon you and overtake you, if you obey the voice of the

Lord your God. You will be blessed in the city
and blessed in the country...you will be blessed
when you come in and blessed when you go out."
(Deuteronomy 28:2-6)

Did Adam go looking for God after he sinned in the
garden or did God go looking for Adam? God seeks out
and reveals Himself to *all* people. We talked about this,
remember? God is not willing that any should perish but
that all would turn to Him. He's seeking you now. Now, as
you read this book, He is revealing Himself to you. Listen
to the words of Jesus.

"For the Son of man has come to seek and to save that
which was lost." Interesting, He says, "*was* lost" instead
of "is" lost. We are no longer lost to God. No one who
will choose His free gift is lost. And, again, He will reveal
Himself to every person...

"The Lord *has made known His salvation*, His
righteousness He has revealed in the sight of the
nations." (Psalm 98:2)

God is not on an undercover mission! He's trying to
get *everyone* saved.

"He *has revealed* His wrath of judgement against
all ungodliness and unrighteousness of men
who suppress the truth... Because, what may
be known of God is manifest (made known,
revealed) in them, *for God has shown it to them.*
For since the creation of the world His invisible
attributes are *clearly seen,* being understood by
the things that are made, even His eternal power
and Godhead, *so that they are without excuse.*"
(Romans 1:18-20)

God is not only seeking *you*. God has set it up so if you seek Him, you *will* find Him.

Jesus said, "Ask and *it will* be given to you, *seek* and *you will* find, knock and the door *will be* opened to you." (Matthew 7:7)

Jeremiah 29:11 is a well-known verse~ "For I know the thoughts I think toward you," says the Lord, "thoughts of peace and not of evil, to give you a future and a hope." But many don't know the verses that follow...

Jeremiah 29:12~ "Then you will call upon Me and go and pray to Me, and *I will listen to you*." 13~ "And you will seek Me and *find Me*, when you search for Me with all your heart." 14~ "*I will be found* by you," says the Lord.

Now, whether you know it or not, that is spoken by a God who cannot lie. (Numbers 23:19)

We may not like the way God has revealed Himself because we want to be let off the hook, as it were. But God has, and does, reveal Himself. If God did openly manifest Himself in all His majestic power and glory in the middle of Times Square, people would give into believing in Him out of fear. But then that's fear, not love.

Proverbs 8:17 makes it clear. "I love those who love Me, and *those who seek Me diligently will find Me*."

Again, the Bible says, "God is Love" (1 John 4:8) The whole of God's message is love. All that He is and does is love. And, someone will say, "Well, I know some things in the Old Testament that God did, and they weren't loving." Remember your kids? Might they say the same thing about some things you did or do that they don't understand? Just because our kids don't get discipline or our righteous judgments doesn't mean we weren't doing those things out of love for them.

One day, they'll grow up and finally understand all we did was out of love. One day we'll *go up* and understand all God did was out of perfect love. Not *to* us, but, *for* us.

The difference between us and Him is He has been to the end of our story. He knows perfectly how it all plays out and therefore can see how everything, even the horrible pain, will be for our benefit.

He has provided every person every chance to know Him and His great love. Study this next truth carefully, will you? See how truly good and in control He is.

> "And He has made from one blood every nation of men to dwell on *all* the face of the earth and has determined their pre-appointed times (*when* you will live on the earth) and the boundaries of their dwellings (*where* you will live on the earth) *so that* (this is why He's done this) *they should seek the Lord*, in the hope that they might grope (reach) for Him *and find Him*, though He is not far from each one of us." (Acts 17:26,27)

God would not be a just God if He sent someone to hell that never had a chance. But I know God is a just God. Everyone will have a chance and a choice to love and accept Him or deny and reject Him, just as you are being given this chance right now. And it's not the volume of knowledge that you acquire. It is the intensity of your search!

And if you search for Him with all your heart- you *will* find Him! You WILL find Him! That's what the Bible says. It's extremely clear!

God is a just God and God is love.

> "For God so loved the world that He gave His only begotten Son, that *whoever* (that includes *you*) believes in Him should not perish but have everlasting life." (John 3:16)

C.S. Lewis makes a brilliant statement. He says, "There are two types of people in the world. The person who bows his knee to God and says, 'Your will be done.' And the person who does not bow his knee to God, and God says, 'Alright, then, *your* will be done.'"

Listen. This is as fair as it gets folks! It can't be any fairer than *this*. God gave you a free will. He reveals Himself to every person. He gave you the ability to choose. Every person will end up in his or her eternal destination exactly where he or she chooses to be... That's fair.

To give you the dignity of freedom and then to violate your free will- *that* would be unjust- and *that* would be unfair. God gives you the privilege and ability to decide where you will spend eternity and to choose whether you will love Him or not.

There's an old saying that speaks with good advice when it comes to love relationships. It goes like this: "If you love someone, set them free. If they return to you, it was meant to be."

This saying declares the truth about love. It must be free. When someone is free to choose and they use that freedom to choose to love you, then, and *only then*, is it true and genuine love.

He has given us freedom. He has made a way for His bride to come home. He pursues us. He pursues *you*! He courts you and romances you! He draws you aside to Himself! In the greatest of sacrifices, He has rescued you and proved His immeasurable love for you!

I'd like to help you understand a perspective concerning God's justice, God's goodness, and God's love, and I'd like to borrow the words of Pastor Robert Morris. He's seen this truth and if you will get this, it will completely change the way you see God.

"God's goodness is so much better than ours. His justice is so much higher than ours. And His love is so much deeper than ours. The only way I can talk about it is analogically. I can only give you an analogy because I cannot tell you how much God really loves you. I cannot express it enough with the language I'm limited to. But let me try..."

"If I say, 'I love you,' and you refuse my love, I hurt, because I've lost something. When God says He loves you, and you refuse *His* love, He hurts. But He hurts because *you've* lost something. It's a completely unselfish love. Listen to me carefully... It's *your* choice. But if you reject His love, you will lose *everything*! You will lose everything- And He knows that."

"Don't get hung up on the fact that there's only one way. Get excited that there *is* a way! Get excited that God has revealed that way to you— His Name is Jesus Christ. Jesus is the only way. But you have a completely free will. You can accept God's love or not. No person, NO person can truthfully say to God, "You are rejecting me." But God can truthfully say to a person, "You are rejecting Me.""

"You see, God didn't want robots. So, God created us as human *beings*. Not human *doings*, but *Beings*. You are a spirit living in a body, but you have a soul that's going to live forever. You have a choice. God *gave* you a choice. God has a will and so because He created you in His image, you also have a will. You can choose to believe in God or not to believe in God."

I really believe you want to choose to believe in God. That's the reason you've read this book through. Something piqued your interest. Something would not allow you to put this book down, but instead, drove you to keep reading. That something could be the Holy Spirit drawing you- drawing you aside to Himself. He's either drawing you to Him for the very first time or drawing you *back* to Himself. Maybe you encountered God when you were younger and He's calling you to come home. Or maybe you've never fully come to Him and called on Him but have been curious and thinking about this for a while.

I want to encourage you right now to settle it. To choose Him. To seek and follow Him. To find out the truth of why you're here. To allow Him to reveal your purpose in this life for the God who loves you.

In your heart, say, "God, I'm coming home. I'm coming back to You. I receive Jesus as my Lord and as my Savior."

I promise you; if you will make a choice to receive Him, He, then, will give you power to become His son or daughter. "To as many as received Him, He then gave the power to become children of God." (John 1:12)

"If you declare with your mouth, "Jesus is Lord,"
and believe in your heart that God raised Him
from the dead, you *will* be saved." (Romans 10:9)

You may be thinking, *"I'll wait. I have time. I'm a mess right now but when I get my life cleaned up, I'll be able to do this."*

It is not your power or ability to change that makes you accepted by God. It is Jesus' sacrificial payment for you and your choice in faith to believe this was done for you which makes you accepted. It's nothing more than accepting a free gift. Once you choose, by your free will, to take His gift, He will come to live within you, and His power will change you from the inside out. (John 17:20-23)

Your enemy attempts to convince you you're not good enough, and it's easy for us to believe this because the truth is, we are not. But *Jesus* is!

It is our belief in our own power which keeps us from the real power. Rebellion says, "I can do this!" Romance says, "It's already done for you." Come and see what the *true* love of your life has already done!

Chapter Eleven

WHAT IS TRUTH?

~⌇

"Some say that the age of chivalry is past, that the spirit of romance is dead. The age of chivalry is never past so long as there is a wrong left unredressed on earth." ~Charles Kingsley

Whether we are believers in God or not, we all enjoy certain aspects of the goodness of God in this earth- Love, relationships, peace, joy, beauty, light, warmth, laughter, new life, etc.

I want you to take a moment and think with me about everything that is *good* about life- Babies, puppies, sunsets, sunrises, waterfalls, beaches, a warm shower on a cold day, a cool shower on a hot day, great food in magical places, mothers, friendship, victories, the butterflies of new love in your tummy, and sweet sleep. The soft touch of the one you love and waking up next to them...

Now, I want you to imagine a place where none of this exists- where no *good* thing is possible. A place that is the absence of all things good. A place without friendship or love or any measure of comfort at all. A place of solitude and utter loneliness that never ends- where not even one pleasant thought will find you. This is separation from God. This place? This place is hell. And this place is as real as real can get.

Wow, Patch! Why would you speak of such things!? Because Jesus did- more than He spoke of anything else.

The Bible asks the question, "For what partnership can righteousness have with wickedness? Or what fellowship does light have with darkness?" (2 Corinthians 6:14)

There was a time when you were *not* living, but there will never be a time again when you will not be alive somewhere and we are headed for one of two places when we leave this world.

In one, no darkness can reside. It is filled with the Light and goodness of God. This place is all the good things listed above and more, multiplied infinitely.

> "There will be no more night. They will not need the light of a lamp or the light of the sun, for the Lord God will be their light. And they will reign for ever and ever." (Revelation 22:5)

In the other place, no light can exist. Jesus called it "Outer darkness." (Matthew 8:12, 22:13, 25:30) It is filled with the darkness of evil and is the absence of even a single fragment or moment of anything that might resemble good. Just as no evil can reside in heaven, no good can reside in hell.

One place is peace, and the other the extreme opposite of peace, which the Bible calls torment. (Luke 16:28) God is not in this place. Therefore, no good is in this place.

Our worst day here on this earth would seem a wonderful paradise from the reality of this place.

This reality reveals why our great and merciful God went to such extremes to defeat and undo this for us. To save us from an eternal existence without Him. Not believing in Jesus does not send you to hell. We are all on course and bound for this destination because of the darkness of sin which entered through Adam and Eve. This darkness is in opposition to God. He cannot be in the presence of evil and not judge and destroy it. Who and what He is dictates, without exception, His complete condemnation and requisite to destroy any form of unrighteousness.

Listen, we don't get a disease because we don't go to the doctor. We go to the doctor because we already have a disease. If we die in our disease because we refuse the doctor's treatment, the doctor cannot be blamed. We are born with the disease of sin, and we are already dying as separated from God.

We hate the cancer which takes so many of our loved ones from us, but we do not hate the person because they have cancer!

Understand this, in order to lovingly give us free will as humans, the possibility we would use that free will to choose against our Creator could not be resolved. Without free will, we would be robotic slaves. Without free will, no genuine love can exist!

This unyielding paradox must be understood before one can begin to question God's integrity or the existence of evil. If God violates our free will to choose *against* Him, there can be no genuine choice *for* Him!

Each person will live eternally in the place of their own choosing. If I duct-taped you to a chair and sought to force you to love me, it would never change the fact you didn't. Your love would only be real if I gave you freedom, and then, you chose to stay. If someone does not want God now, they will not want Him in heaven, and God will not force anyone to be with Him against their will.

God is not willing that *any* should perish. Therefore, He will allow tragedy to befall someone, because some people will only turn to Him in brokenness. This is what we talked about, "tough love." I'd rather my son experience prison than to destroy any hope he might have for a future by overdosing on drugs. Out of these two alternatives, I will, in love, choose the lesser pain for the greater good.

What is truth? The truth is this, God loves you. The truth is God knows you. He knows precisely what it will take to bring you to Him and to secure you with Him for eternity. There is nothing He will not allow into your life to turn your will to choose Him.

He also knows those who, no matter what, will never choose Him. Remember, He is not bound by time and space. He has seen how it all plays out. He knows who are His—who will choose Him. Not that He has predetermined that some will, and some will not, but because He has been to the end of the story and seen the outcome. He has seen exactly what it will take for each one to come to the place where they may choose Him. So, again, how you get to heaven, the amount of discipline or tough love or tragedy, is not what matters to God. He will allow the pressure and fire it will take to save you. For His ultimate goal is to ensure that you will not (hear me-you WILL not) perish apart from Him.

The truth is, we are not shown the whole picture. If we're honest, even as Christians, we often feel that we are not shown enough. This is why God is God. I wish I had a better answer for you. Perhaps this must be a part of what distinguishes us from God.

Why the hiddenness of God? We will dive a bit deeper into this shortly but for now, I can speculate that it is to do with the sacrifice of faith. I could speculate that If God were completely transparent, there would be no need to trust Him, and if there were no *need* to trust Him, then how would we ever know we could?

I could speculate if God were to show up in all His glory, people would bow down and believe in fear, rather than love. People might choose Him, not out of love but in fear! What kind of good relationship is based on fear? Maybe He stays hidden for the sake of love?

We could speculate, because of what we know of His character He wants intimacy with His people. After all, He didn't shout His power and majesty over us and above us, but instead chose to come down and become one of us. To kneel down beside us. To hold us. To heal us. To experience this life and what it means to be human *with* us. And then to die for us? How could we be intimate with someone we feared, or thought could never relate to us?

We must speculate to some extent, though, because the truth is, we don't fully know His reasons. But the more I get to know Him, by the way He's chosen to interact with us, and for all the ways I've just discussed, I am convinced that those reasons are born out of love for me, and they are sincere.

One of the great enigmas of humanity is how men will justify their own reason in their questioning of God's character, while fully aware of the weakness of their own. They peek through a tiny keyhole into a vast and complex room and presume to know all its contents.

They stand proud on the deck of a ship, built with the brilliance of their minds and the strength of their backs. Through mighty storms, they land on a distant shore to shower themselves with accolades. Conquerors, they are called! Conquerors of the distance between two worlds—between two fine lines in the palm of God's hand! Then, taking the feather of God's bird to the ink of God's plant, they cover the paper of God's tree with philosophies that question His power.

Men will go to the ends of the earth in a breathtaking display of chivalry and romance to win the thief of their heart. They will give up their very soul for the woman they love, considering it an honor to die for her. Then, while still intoxicated by her God-given scent, his pounding heart cannot steady the shaky quill soon enough to pen the proclamation that there is no such love in God!

Perfect wisdom requires meekness—power under control. Because God controls His power for the ultimate good, men assume Him powerless.

Perfect love allows folly's pain to correct and restore for the benefit of the loved. Because God allows these fires of purification, men assume Him heartless.

It is His greatest quality, or that for which I am most grateful, that amazes me most. The patience or grace with which He somehow bears these evil thoughts of men and their insatiable lust to print them, is astonishing. For me, this is the true mystery! It is only when I look on my sleeping son, with his hateful words of rebellion still stinging my ears, that I can begin to grasp it.

Oh, what a broken jewel, a poisonous flower is the human heart. Able to bless and curse with the same tongue. Indeed, in the same breath! Able to pen such beauty and still murder the masses. To climb the highest peak and then wallow in the mired pit.

How very strange is the contradiction of the heart of man. What hypocrisy to employ the frailty of the human mind to question the integrity of an infinite God. Under the staggering and humiliating weight of all his miscalculations and negated theories, he can still muster the arrogance to believe in the conclusions of his own imaginative wisdom.

With the mind his Creator has graciously given him, he formulates ignorant and futile reasonings to seek to condemn a perfect God in order to justify the choices of his imperfection. Foolishly, he attributes and imposes his flawed character upon a God he does not know. With blind eyes and a withered hand, he points toward a mortal truth with no boundaries and no anchor and then faults God that he is adrift.

It is not that he seeks reason or sound logic, but excuse. An admission of any righteous standard robs him of what he sees as freedom. To protect that perception, he must deny the standard. And to do this, he must discredit the belief and guardian of any standard standing in opposition to that life he has predetermined himself to embrace.

Understand what I am presenting here. It is the child telling the parent how the world should work—what is fair and unfair. It is the immature heart of the child protesting a curfew, or the rights to friends who engage in destructive behavior. To live in his own world, with his own rules, free from consequence. He sees your rules as bondage—a threat to his freedom.

Is the twelve-year-old justified by his reasoning? Or is his adolescent mind clouded by his immaturity? Is he right simply because he believes himself to be so? Is the truth affected when he fails to understand it? Of course not.

The truth is not affected by reasonings, protest, manipulation, or lack of comprehension. No matter how long or "effective" the argument, truth remains unmoved. We do not have to like it for it to be true. Our errored opinions, however well-presented will never do anything to manipulate truth. They only serve to manipulate ourselves. Truth holds a power that will defend itself, and no amount of clever wordplay or passion or diligent preparation can bring down the truth. Like the mountain obscured by the low-lying clouds, it may be hidden for the moment, but it is still there, solid and immutable.

There is a giant rock sitting just offshore at a place called "Neah Bay" on the farthest northwest coast of Washington State. It's one of the most magical places I've ever been. Over several millennia this rock has been pounded by the pressure of countless waves and powerful storms. Yet it remains unmoved. Though the weaker parts of the massive structure have been swept away, this has only revealed a truer representation of itself. The moveable has been washed away, while the true and unchangeable core remains.

Men will always be the weakness and perishable elements of truth. The flawed musings of our imaginations may accumulate on the rock of truth and those parts are subject to the waves and storms of those who seek to dismantle it. But the truth of God is solid, complete, immoveable, and eternal.

Man can bring all he dares to bear on this truth, and all he has will never begin to remove a grain from the eternal rock of the word of God. The very fact this idea emerges at all is evidence such an endeavor is born in fragility and foolishness.

So, you have a God whose wisdom you cannot fathom, and you see this as a bad thing? Would you have a god with the mind of men? With the strength of men? With the character and wisdom of men? Then you would have no God at all!

We could have no peace in the knowledge of a god we could fully understand. We could have no hope in a god who did not transcend the life he created. For then, he could hold no power over that life, or over death.

"But who are you, a human being, to talk back to (question) God? Shall what is formed say to the One who formed it, 'Why did you make me like this?'" (Romans 9:20)

Instead of trying to make sense of what we cannot, we should be listening to that which He has made clear.

"For My thoughts are not your thoughts, neither are your ways My ways," declares the LORD. "As the heavens are higher than the earth, so are My ways higher than your ways and My thoughts than your thoughts." (Isaiah 55:8-9)

What is crystal clear in God's word is this: God is Holy. We are not. Without His help, we will perish. Because of the darkness of our condition, which the Bible calls sin, we cannot live in the presence of God. He has reconciled this problem by entering our existence as Christ Jesus to stand in our place and take the penalty for this sin upon Himself.

Our faith in this act of love is what frees us from the charge which was against us and places us in right standing with our Holy God, able to escape separation from God, and instead, reside in His presence for eternity.

Adam had a choice. He chose to rebel. He received death.

Jesus had a choice. He chose to obey. He received life.

We have a choice. Agree with Adam and choose death and separation from God and all goodness, or, agree with and choose Christ Jesus and choose eternal life in the presence of God and all goodness.

It's funny. People want a miracle. But they don't want to be in a trial that requires a miracle.

People want to be rich, but they don't like that it takes hard work to get there. They wish it were easier.

People want to be in shape, but they don't like that it takes hard work to be in shape. They wish it were easier.

People want a great relationship, but they don't want to put in the hard work it takes to actually have one. They wish it were easier.

People want to have great kids, but they don't like that it takes hard work and time to raise them. They wish it were easier.

People want to go to heaven, but they don't like that it simply takes faith to get there... They wish it were harder.

Harder is so much easier for us to understand, therefore, so much easier for us to believe.

What they don't see is heaven's door was not easily opened. It took a man through unspeakable agony, not just physically, but spiritually. It took the courage of an innocent man to choose (and be sure, He chose it) to endure an excruciating punishment that we, the guilty, deserved. Hear me—your Way to heaven's eternity came at the greatest of costs. It cost your God the most precious thing to Him—His Son.

So, is it too good to be true? *Or*, are you missing how truly hard it was to accomplish this amazing good?

Once you see the cost of this *Way*; once you feel the weight of this *Truth*; once you realize the sacrifice of this one *Life;* you can only arrive at one conclusion, one reason it seems to be too good to be true... Love.

Love, true love was the power that swung open the guarded gates of heaven. And it was not, by any stretch of the imagination, easy.

The truth is, many have claimed deity, but no other person in human history has ever proved himself to be God the way Jesus has.

No other person is said to have performed the miracles that Jesus did.

No other person ever raised people from the dead or foretold of his death, burial, and resurrection with such boldness and accuracy.

And this Person, Jesus of Nazareth, claimed to be the *only* Way to heaven.

So, each of us, including you, must come to terms with this and make a decision concerning what you will do with Jesus. In light of His claims, and the claims of those who knew Him, and have testified as witnesses to His divinity, you must come to one of three conclusions.

Either Jesus was a liar, a lunatic, or He was Lord of all creation.

Either, he was a master of deceit, the likes of which the world has never known before or since, convincing those who knew Him and generations to come to go to their deaths in support of Him.

Or, He was a madman, cunning enough to mask His insanity so that thousands somehow missed it.

Or He was, and is, exactly who He claimed to be—God.

One day, whichever one of these is reality, the truth *will* be known. If he was a liar or a lunatic, you may never know the difference. *But,* if He is Lord, the God and Creator of the world and your soul, then everything He ever said will also be true.

My dear friend, in light of this very sobering thought, I would suggest you take all information afforded you into careful consideration before reaching your final conclusion.

Listen, you will know soon enough. If you will seek Him, call to Him, read about who He is, and spend a little time in pursuit of Him, you will find that amazing moment, that unexplainable union, that indescribable knowing, and the most splendid revelation that He has always been pursuing you!

There is a sweet fragrance which has floated down the corridors of time, capturing all who catch the scent of her. There is nothing else quite like her. She is pure and bright, and her aroma brings instant peace to the souls who have embraced her. She is wisdom, and she is carried on the very breath of God. One day, the wind of the Spirit of Truth will blow over you my friend, and you will come face to face with the Truth. And He will take your heart, as you take His hand, and you will forever turn your eyes toward Him. For there you will have been and there you will always long to be.

Chapter Twelve

HEAD TO HEART

⸎

"The rebel can never find peace. He knows what is good and, despite himself, does evil. The value which supports him is never given to him once and for all." ~Albert Camus

G race seems to be all anyone (or many churches) wants to talk about these days.

I get it. The message of the coming judgment, obedience, and dying to self, may seem to be something out of date- a stumbling block to those considering Christianity.

Apparently, it seems to some, in light of all that surrounds us concerning the signs of the approaching return of Christ, that it's important to draw people toward something more attractive, more pleasant, and especially today, less offensive. It seems it might be more effective to adjust the "sales strategy." Any good marketing plan requires a good hook, right?

The problem is grace without contrast devalues the very truth of grace. There is a reason grace is amazing and omission or dilution of that reason leaves a hollow and muddied reflection of its splendor. Understand, curious unbelievers take full note of this. Our love affair with grace lacks any depth or sincerity if our heart is not wrenched by the pain and sacrifice endured to produce it and the willingness to heed the call to share in those sufferings.

"And if we are children, then we are heirs: heirs of God and co-heirs with Christ; if indeed we suffer with Him, so that we may also be glorified with Him." (Romans 8:17)

We simply skim over it to embrace its results and so traverse our need and ability to relate to God. We cannot become more like Him while callously continuing to greedily take from Him. As Christians, we must not trivialize the weight or scope of sin. In some ways, we are engaging in the same self-deception as the unbeliever, going through our daily lives thinking sin to be something that will not affect us.

I am convinced man's greatest weakness is actually one of his most powerful abilities—the ability to rationally excuse himself from that which is glaringly obvious to him, even while completely certain of the adverse consequences of his decision. Humans have the depraved propensity and power to rationalize themselves into or out of a truth they have already determined and accepted as settled. No matter how inevitably dire the result, or how plain their own experience has made it, they will find a self-patronizing loophole which allows them, in the lust of the moment, to abandon reason.

This is the inescapable torment of sin—to possess, unequivocally, the knowledge of good and evil, yet pathetically unable to raise a significant defense against our own perverse rationalization of the two. This was the outcome of Eden. This *"Self"* is the problem which can never remedy itself. Thankfully, gracefully, we are not left to this paradox.

Many believers choose to see sin as powerless. Through their skewed view of grace, they become passively and dangerously confident concerning compromise.

Therefore, they are uncomfortable with a message that confronts this complacency on Sunday morning, or even in the moment at hand. "Grace covers my sin! Why can't we just focus on the grace of God and get away from all this sin stuff?" As Dr. David Jeremiah writes in his revelatory work, *The Book of Signs*, "Before we ignore sin and bask in the grace of God, we need to hear these words from theologian Cornelius Plantinga Jr:"

> "To speak of grace without sin is... to trivialize the cross of Jesus Christ, to skate past all the struggling by good people down the ages, to forgive, accept, and rehabilitate sinners, including themselves, and therefore to cheapen the grace of God that always comes to us with blood on it. What had we thought the ripping and writhing on Golgotha were all about?

> "To speak of grace without looking squarely at these realities, without painfully honest acknowledgement of our own sin and its effects is to shrink grace to a mere embellishment of the music of creation, to shrink it down to a mere grace note.

> "In short, for the Christian church (even its recently popular seeker services) to ignore,

euphemize, or otherwise mute the lethal reality of sin is to cut the nerve of the gospel. For the sober truth is that without full disclosure on sin, the gospel of grace becomes impertinent, unnecessary, and finally uninteresting."

You see, there is hardly a moment when grace reaches or arrives in us in its truest magnificent form as when we are brokenly aware of how desperate and unworthy we are to receive it. It is, as Plantinga puts it (and I paraphrase), like splicing out that one climactic moment of a song apart from the emotionally competing and defining polarity in the overture and totality of the rest of the piece.

We love the greatest when fearfully aware we might never have found it. When we realize all our Beloved has endured and conquered just to be with us; when we are unable to take love for granted.

The human soul has a destructive tendency to bury any thought which may challenge the confidence it thinks necessary for success. The longer pride goes unchecked, the easier it becomes to rely on it and the less we see our need for grace. We reach a place in our spiritual walk when we say, "I've got this."

Plantinga writes in *Not the Way it's Supposed to Be:*

"Self-deception about our sin is a narcotic, a tranquilizing and disorienting suppression of our spiritual central nervous system. What's devastating about it is that when we lack an ear for wrong notes in our lives, we cannot play right ones or even recognize them in the performance of others... Moral beauty begins to bore us. The idea that the human race needs a Savior sounds quaint."

This truth is anything but quaint. Grace *is* amazing! Not because it allows us to become cavalier regarding sin, but because it saves us, continually, from even our arrogant proclivity to blatantly repackage it for ourselves in order to feel the freedom to abandon its very purpose—to glorify God in perennial dependence on Him and to share Him with others.

I am often brought to my knees as I am ashamedly aware though I have been given the wisdom to see a great deal of the full and imminent fate of those who don't know God, I bounce about my day with no sense of urgency, paying no mind to the issue which breaks my Lord's heart in every moment.

> "Therefore, whoever knows the right thing to do,
> and fails to do it, for him it is sin." (James 4:17)

If I didn't sin in any other way, I need grace for the apathy I often show to the people around me who stand to perish. To ignore our sin is to then become blind to the horror that awaits those who don't know the grace of God. It's disgustingly indefensible to know the city will demolish a condemned building and do nothing to warn the family residing there.

Grace is beautiful and amazing! But only in contrast to the insidious effect and imminent threat of sin—only when seen while *we* sling the whip, and *we* drive the nails into our Savior's flesh. Only in the full revelation of *our* part in sin's heartbreaking reality and deadly consequence can we genuinely share in the truth and power of grace. Do you ever ask yourself the question, "What is wrong with me?"

Why, knowing the right thing to do, do I insist on doing the wrong thing?

Why is it, when we stand at the precipice of a choice we've been faced with many times over that we, once again, choose the way which we know will land us in a pit of regret?

What is it about these temptations that we are so very willing to endure their inevitable consequence? What is it about *us* that almost craves the heartache of desperation? Is it the same reason we use drugs and alcohol—the same reason some people cut themselves? Could it be that we just simply want to feel something? Could it be, at some point, it doesn't even matter what that something is? Are we so dissatisfied with ourselves we are unable to find happiness in peace? Or, are we so without peace we are dissatisfied with our idea of happiness?

This cycle is the human condition that lies between expectation and fulfillment of that expectation. Where does this expectation come from? Why do we have it?

There is one more thing I want to share with you before I leave you with your thoughts about all this.

Though God seems hidden, and many try to contend that there is no way we can fully know the truth, God has not hidden the truth from us.

He pleads with us to engage our heart and mind to see creation and the logic of order in this world through reason, and to recognize the need of the human heart to fill a void which no earthly provision is able.

He calls us to set aside our inclination to reject and abhor the idea of accountability for sin, to trivialize it or ignore it. Just for a moment, turn this intrinsic idea on its head and remember that justice (Right's triumph over wrong) is not only reasonable but essential.

Remember that it is also our nature to require justice. Remember that it is our responsible duty to discipline our children's wrong behavior for their good and the good of the world. Remember that in their inability to understand our ways, and the wisdom behind our ways, they cannot always see the transforming necessity of justice or accountability, and their immature, incomplete vision of this principle does not invalidate its integrity.

Simply denying a truth because we don't like the way it makes us feel will never negate it as authentic or disqualify it as necessary. Instead of looking at the fact that wrong (sin) will be judged, look at the way God has graciously chosen to reconcile that judgment. Look at the hope!

"Come now and let us reason together," says the Lord, "Though your sins are as scarlet, they will be white as snow. Though they are like crimson, they will be like wool. If you are willing and obedient, you will eat the good things of the land." (Isaiah 1:18-19)

God says, "Let's talk about this! Yes, there must be justice and I have made a way through it. Not over, under or around it, but through it. So that you will know I am a God of *justice*! And I have paid the price and consequence for you *Myself*, so that you may know I am a God of *mercy*!"

He not only shows His perfectly balanced handling of the human dilemma, but God invites you into the multi-layered architectural order and perfect cohesiveness in the truths revealed throughout the stories of God and His creation.

Mystery. Such an incredible word! It's one of our favorite delicacies in this world. We love stories of mystery—the mystery in relationships, the mystery of science and creation and the mystery of the unknown. The very mention of the word instantly piques our interest and draws us in!

Mystery is defined: "Something that is difficult or impossible to understand or explain." What do you think would be the key word in this definition? You might be inclined to say, "difficult" or "impossible" or you may think it's about "understanding."

But the key word for this application is "Something." Before there can be a need for explanation or understanding, there must be a *something* to explain. There must be an undeniable something that presents itself rooted in reality before one can consider its nature, origin, purpose or reason. No one needs to explain nothing.

Albert Einstein said, "The most incomprehensible thing about the world is that it is comprehensible."

He also wrote the following in 1932:

"The most beautiful and deepest experience a man can have is the sense of the mysterious. It's the underlying principle of religion as well as of all serious endeavor in art and science. He who never had this experience seems to me, if not dead, then at least blind.

"To sense that behind anything that can be experienced there is a *something* that our minds cannot grasp, whose beauty and sublimity reaches us only indirectly, this is religiousness. In this sense, I am religious.

"To me it suffices to wonder at these secrets and to attempt humbly to grasp with my mind a mere image of the lofty structure of all there is."

Einstein's religious views have been widely studied and often misunderstood. At one point, he did state he believed in the pantheistic god of Baruch Spinoza. He did not believe in a personal God who concerns Himself with the fates and actions of human beings. A view he described as naïve.

Naïve is an interesting word. It assumes a general sense that certain assumptions can be and are indeed a given in the realm of knowledge. That is, one can only attribute naivety to a person who falls short of some obvious standard of higher reason in a given subject of thought. They are innocently missing something known by experience. It's an assumption of assumptions.

The person who states an opinion to be naïve is standing from a position of the assumed authority of his own opinion, or as to what is the commonly accepted experience or perspective of mankind, without the consideration of what yet may be discovered and added to that experience.

In light of the last sentence of Einstein's statement, "Wondering at these *secrets*, I humbly *attempt* to grasp with my mind a mere image of all there is." I find it counter-intuitive (or naïve) to use the word naïve in addressing the unknown.

Einstein has vehemently asserted his belief that this world of order must have a designer. To then admit he is humbly attempting to grasp what that may mean completely, stands in opposition to the view that the God he admittedly does not know could not be personal or concerned or involved, or that the person who believes in a personal God would in any way be naïve.

The point, however, of sharing Einstein's words with you is to touch on what many mistakenly reduce to curiosity, but which is a much deeper pillar in the foundation of the human spirit. Einstein called it "the most beautiful and deepest experience a person can have." "The sense of the mysterious." He considered anyone who has never experienced this as either "dead or blind."

"To sense that behind anything that can be experienced, there is a something that our minds cannot grasp, who's beauty and sublimity reaches us only indirectly (or incompletely)." *(Insert mine)*

There are really only two kinds of people when it comes to these mysteries: those who want to know and those who don't. Those who are on a quest for truth and those whose truth reaches no further than the limits of self. Those who are unafraid of what the truth may reveal and those who are afraid of it. Those with courage and those with cowardice.

There are atheists with whom I've debated that when asked the question, "If Christianity were true, would you believe?" have emphatically said "No."

This reveals the true nature behind their opposition or attack on Christianity. They don't want it to be true. Anyone who is on a sincere and relentless pursuit of truth would never make that statement. Only those who are apathetic or hostile toward anything that might contradict their chosen lifestyle would. They are not on a truth quest, but a happiness quest. It's not an intellectual issue, but a heart issue.

> *"The heart of the human problem is the problem of the human heart."* ~Adrian Rogers

So, I ask you, do you want to know the truth? Are you on a sincere and relentless search for it? If Christianity were true, would *you* believe?

How could it hurt you to learn the truth? What is it *you* are afraid of?

Are you, as I was, afraid of how you might feel? Are you afraid, somehow, it will make you some kind of social weirdo? Are you afraid you will no longer be invited to the party? Are you afraid if you discover the truth, you won't be able to have fun?

Remember, "God has not given us a spirit of fear, but of power and love, and of a sound mind." (2 Timothy 1:7)

Fear is from the enemy of truth, the enemy of understanding. And with fear, he seeks to rob us of power, love, and self-control.

Listen. The Truth will set you free—free from weakness, free from worry, free from hate, free from stress and the longing for peace and fulfillment. It will set you free from the consequence of sin and the emptiness it always brings. It will set you free to truly love and be courageous.

> "You will know the truth, and the truth will set you free." (John 8:32)

Like I always say, don't take my word for it. Search out the truth for yourself. The worst thing that can happen is you will discover what you believe and what you don't.

You are either a person with the courage to wonder about these secrets enough to investigate them for yourself, or you are content to remain in ignorance, afraid of what an investigation might reveal.

The romantic heart seeks to pursue the mystery of love. The romantic heart takes chances. It is not satisfied with anything less than what's real, and it reaches for what it knows it needs—at any risk.

The rebel heart refuses anything outside the walls it erects for itself, and in foolish pride, proclaims its independent allegiance to a stubbornly blind commitment to fortify those walls.

Which heart do *you* have?

The juxtaposition should be obvious—though we are thoroughly convicted within ourselves of what's good and just, and altogether right, our nature's propensity to follow an instinct of rebellious self-deception to an end which abandons these enduring virtues leaves us wanting for an external solution. And with that revelation, to accept there must be one. And with that, a search.

In other words, we are perpetually pulled in two opposing directions: good and evil. If it were only good, there would be no problem to consider. If it were only evil, we would not be aware of the problem. We are born with the problem and fully aware of it. The fact we reject a solution to the problem while admitting there is one, reveals that we are so captivated by evil we are willing to trade the temporary pleasure found in it for the opportunity to escape its consequence. This is the nature which prevents our communion or relationship with God. We recognize our need for good but are in constant communion or relationship with evil.

God not only will not, but cannot, abide the presence of evil.

The romantic heart seeks loyalty, commitment, honesty and devotion, and there are no limits on what the romantic heart is willing to sacrifice to obtain and sustain this precious rectitude. The romantic will not endure a divided, half-hearted relation with anyone. The romantic will not endure a lie, for it cancels and completely destroys the image and value of what was or might be.

The rebel heart is so consumed with itself as to refuse a total commitment or connection to any one person or thing. It takes from all that surrounds it. It is comfortable with deceit. The rebel uses. They view everything through a selective lens of self-preservation, assuming everything a competitor in a game in which giving equals losing. The romantic looks for ways to lift others up and the rebel tears down to elevate themselves.

The romantic lives in perpetual hope in the power of sacrificial love. The rebel lives in hoarding fear and their own ability to manipulate that love for a perverted sense of power. The rebel will pretend a superficial, emotional interest or socially acceptable virtue until he has come to the place it will cost him. Then suddenly he exposes his true motive. He doesn't trust because trust could cost him.

It will seem that the rebel has won, but in truth, the integrity and sincerity of the romantic cannot be diminished, therefore costs him nothing. While the rebel has taken a monetary prize, he has walked away without acquiring that which was of infinite worth. Again, and again the rebel comes face to face with the greatest of life's treasures and steals away with little more than a mere image of the beauty of probity. With counterfeit contentment, he will tuck this image into his bag of manipulative tools and carry it into his next conquest.

The rebel heart is blinded to the fact he is serving a much bigger agenda than himself. The spirit of his heart's motivation is an ancient one, born in pride and grown in Eden's infamous con. The romantic's heart is also ancient and seeks the truth which overcomes this con. It is eternal and is expressed fully in the sacrifice of Calvary.

We are serving one of two great purposes. That of the romantic heart of the God of truth or the deceitful rebel heart of Satan. And make no mistake; these opposing forces each carry their "rewards" with them.

Which will you choose? This, whether you know it or not, is *the question* of your life.

Is it a mystery? Only as much as you choose it to be. How high are your walls? They are as high as you seek to serve yourself. With each brick you remove from the wall of self, the truth of the mystery shines clearer and brighter into your life.

If you take nothing else from this book, let it be this: Make a decision to answer the questions of your heart. Choose now, in this moment, to discover the truth for yourself. Make a covenant or pact with yourself to embark on a relentless pursuit of the reality of the mystery of life.

Put down your devices for a time and take up the greatest quest of the human heart. Break free of your rebel chains and awaken the bold spirit of romance within you!

Slay the coward of conformity which bores you, bleeds you, and binds your restless wings. Listen to that rising cry beneath your chest, fighting to get out. Rebel against rebellion, board your ship, and leave your tiny island. Raise your sails and call the winds of truth to propel you into clarity and purpose. "If any of you lacks wisdom, you should ask God, who gives generously to all without finding fault, and it will be given to you." (James 1:5)

If you're already saved by His grace, you may not realize it, but you have been chosen to impact eternity, not just to enjoy it. This is the greatest privilege of them all. To be called by the Creator of the universe to partner with Him in the greatest story of love the world has ever known.

He calls you to kneel before your King and let Him lay upon your shoulder the sword of the Spirit to knight you as a soldier and a son or daughter. Allow Him to reveal His kingdom to you and His plan for you concerning your place and purpose in it. Decide *now* to refuse to stop searching until you have seen it all. Decide *now* that you will no longer settle for less than all He has for you. Decide *now* to shed and burn the fool's cloak of rebellion. Decide *today* to clothe yourself in the righteous robe of the King and take up your sword for His cause. Decide *in this moment* to conquer ignorance and discover the truth your enemy has fought so hard to keep from you. Call on the Holy Spirit to pull back the curtain and then step into a power and peace you could never have imagined!

Fear that you will lose control is all that holds you back, because faith in His control is where the power lies. Jesus said, "My power is made perfect (complete) in (your) weakness." (2 Corinthians 12:9)

> "He who loves his life (controlling it to serve himself) will lose it, and he who hates his life in this world (placing God above it) will keep it for eternal life." (John 12:25)

We will either choose to live this life in our power or in His. Once you've understood this, you will wonder how you would have chosen any other way but Him. My friend, I plead with you to see what He is offering you!

> "But to all who believed Him and accepted Him, He gave the right to become children of God. They are reborn, not with a physical birth resulting from human passion or plan, but a birth that comes from God." (John 1:12-13)

You are precious. More than any other thing, I want you to see this truth- that you are precious to God. People are not just precious "corporately" to God, but *you* are specifically, individually, personally, precious to God.

Follow me for a moment in Luke 15:

> "Then all the tax collectors and the sinners drew near to Him (Jesus) to hear Him. And the Pharisees and scribes complained, saying, 'This Man receives sinners and eats with them.' So (in response) He spoke this parable to them saying: 'What man of you, having a hundred sheep, if he loses one of them, does not leave the ninety-nine in the wilderness and go after the one that was lost until he finds it? And when he has found it, he lays it on his shoulders rejoicing. And when

he comes home, he calls together his friends and neighbors, saying to them, 'Rejoice with me, for I have found my sheep which was lost!' I say to you that likewise, there will be more joy in heaven over one sinner who repents than over ninety-nine just persons who need no repentance.'" (Luke 15:1-7)

Obviously, the Shephard in this parable is Jesus. Jesus said clearly, "I am the good Shephard. The good Shephard gives His life for the sheep." (John 10:11)

Understand, the Lord wants you to hear this- You are precious! You! Individually!

Think about this, this Shephard has a hundred sheep. He loses *one*, and He goes after *that one*. He said, "Rejoice with Me because *My* sheep that was lost, I have found." Also see the Shephard doesn't send someone else to find the sheep. He comes *Himself*. He is personally involved. Look at other places where this is shown.

Hebrews 1:3— "...when He had by *Himself* purged our sins..." Hebrews 2:18— "...He, *Himself* has suffered..." Hebrews 13:5— "...He, *Himself* has said, 'I will never leave you nor forsake you.'" Isaiah 59:16— "He saw that there was no man and wondered that there was no intercessor (to bring God and man together); therefore, *His own arm* brought salvation..."

Here is what I want you to know. Jesus *Himself* came to get you!

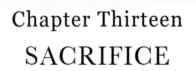

Chapter Thirteen

SACRIFICE

"There's only one effectively redemptive sacrifice, the sacrifice of self will to make room for the knowledge of God." ~Aldous Huxley

I heard a story told by Robert Morris that reminds us of what the Lord did for us.

"After WWI, the United States allocated funds for the orphans in Europe. At one of the orphanages, a very old and thin man brought in a very thin little girl and said, 'I'd like you to take in and take care of my little girl, please.'

"They asked him if she was his daughter, and when he said yes, they said, 'We're very sorry, but our rules are that we can't take in any children if either of the parents are still living.' He said,

'But I've been in prison camps and now I'm too old and too sick to work. She'll die if you don't take care of her.'

"They felt compassion, but they told him they couldn't do anything about it. Then the man said, 'Are you telling me, that if I die, you will take care of my little girl, and she can live and have food, and have clothes and have a home?' And they said, 'Yes.'

"And the father reached down, pulled her up to himself, hugged her, kissed her, and then put her hand in the hand of the man at the desk, and then said to him, 'I'll arrange it.' And he walked out of the orphanage and he hung himself.

The reason I told you that story is because, essentially, that is what Jesus did. I think Jesus said to the Father, "You mean, if I die, they can live." And the Father said, "Yes." And He put my hand in the hand of the Father, and said, "I'll arrange it."

The Shephard left heaven to get *you*. That is how very precious *you* are to Him.

"God is love." (1 John 4:8)

There is a love which we can only understand by experiencing it through the Spirit of God.

Think about this for a minute. Think of our five senses: sight, smell, hearing, taste, and touch. Now love is probably the most powerfully felt sense a human can have but it is not listed in the senses of the human body. Because practically, it is intangible.

Think now about the fact that any of the five senses we recognize can be lost to us. There are blind people, deaf people, people who cannot smell or taste and a condition by which certain people even lose the sensation of touch. While these conditions are unfortunate and I feel for anyone suffering from one or more of them, the fact they are without these abilities does nothing to change the reality of the world around them. Simply because one is unable to feel, hear, smell, taste or see something does not mean the realities of that something is not known or experienced by others.

Yet this is precisely what many who have yet to know God will claim. How very naïve to dismiss the reality of something because you lack the ability to see it or have not yet experienced it. Like the deaf man who disputes what the blind man heard or the blind man what the deaf man saw, we insist on invalidating a reality for which we lack the faculties, or the patience, to know. The caterpillar calls his brother a fool for thinking he will fly one day.

There is a mystery which the apostle Paul said, "has been kept hidden for ages and generations past, but now it has been revealed to God's people." (Colossians 1:26) It's called a mystery because only the people of God, through His Spirit's revelation, can see it.

He said, "To them God has chosen to make known among the Gentiles (Those who don't know) the glorious riches of this mystery, which is Christ in you, the hope of glory." (Colossians 1:27)

The blind person cannot see, the deaf cannot hear, and the one without the Spirit of God cannot experience or understand the things of God.

"The person without the Spirit does not accept the things that come from the Spirit of God but considers them foolishness and cannot understand them because they are discerned (seen) only through the Spirit." (1 Corinthians 2:14)

I mean no offense toward the blind or deaf or otherwise impaired person. But I think most of them would be happy to receive their sight or hearing or to have whatever impairment healed. In a physical sense they might feel incomplete. Before we receive Christ and the Holy Spirit, we are incomplete—lacking our sixth sense you could say. Lacking the ability to see with the wisdom of the Spirit the totality of our being and the world outside the parameters of our other senses, we are not whole.

You would think this would be of interest to people, especially scientists and those whose life has been dedicated to, as Einstein put it, "Grasping the secrets of the structure of all there is."

But "The heart is deceitful above all things and beyond cure. Who can understand it?" (Jeremiah 17:9)

The heart, the rebel heart, is deceitful and beyond cure, at least any human cure. But "with God, all things are possible." (Mark 10:27) For the true romantic, this statement rings true in the deepest parts of us. So often we rebel against love, because so often it hurts. But there is One in whom we need never fear. One whose love will not cost us in the end, because it cost Him. One who will never leave us nor forsake us. One Who "So loved the world that He gave His only begotten Son, that whosoever believes in Him shall not perish but have everlasting life." (John 3:16)

All we want in life is to love and to be loved. From the time we are born, we are infatuated with the idea of love. We are in love with love. Our world searches everywhere for love. We spend all our time searching for love in people. We want to be accepted and feel like we belong to something.

Have you ever wondered why this is true? Or why we continue to attempt to find it even after we have suffered through heartache as a result of love. Even the hardened rebel heart will give it one more try in the right set of circumstances.

> "If I find in myself a desire which no experience in this world can satisfy, the most probable explanation is that I was made for another world."
> ~C.S. Lewis

Yes, we were made to love and for love. There is a reason that no love we find in this world ever truly satisfies us. There is a love we are made for beyond this world that we will forever chase until we find it. There is only One who holds the key to our hearts. And that key unlocks all that we long for in life.

If God is love, and love is what we are all searching for, then we are all searching for God. I am no longer searching for love. I have found it. All my life I would find "love" only to watch it slip through my fingers again to relive the heartache of that loss.

Soren Kierkegaard, a renowned Danish philosopher of the 19th century, tells a story of the kind of love we all long for and it reveals the One who offers us this love. This story also reveals what true romance is about—sacrifice.

David Jeremiah retells this story as only he can:

> "Imagine there was a king who loved a humble maiden. She had no royal pedigree, no education, no standing in the royal court. She dressed in

rags. She lived in a hovel; she lived the ragged life of a peasant. But for reasons no one could quite figure out, the king fell in love with this girl in the way that kings sometimes do. Why he should love her was beyond explaining, but love her he did, and he could not stop loving her.

"One day there awoke in the heart of the king an anxious thought: 'How in the world is he going to reveal his love to this girl? How could he bridge the chasm that separated the two of them?'

"His advisors, of course, told him that all he had to do was command her to become his queen, and it would be done. For he was a man of immense power, every statesman feared his wrath, every foreign power trembled before him, and every courtier groveled in the dust at the king's voice.

"This poor peasant girl would have no power to resist. She would have to become the queen!

"But power, even unlimited power, cannot command love. The king could force her body to be present in the palace, but he could not force love to be present in her heart. He might be able to gain her obedience this way, but coerced submission is not what he wanted. He longed for intimacy of heart and oneness of spirit, and all the power in the world cannot unlock the human heart. It must be opened from within.

"So, he met with his advisors once again and they suggested he try to bridge the chasm by elevating her to his position. He could shower her with gifts, dress her in purple and silk, and have her crowned the queen.

"But if he brought her to his palace, if he radiated the sun of his magnificence over her, if she saw all the wealth, pomp, and power of his greatness, then she would be overwhelmed. How would he ever know if she loved him for himself, or for all that he had given her? And how could she know that he loved her, and would love her still if she had remained only a humble peasant? Would she be able to summon confidence enough never to remember what the king only wished to forget—that he was the king and she had been a humble maiden?

"Every alternative he came up with came to nothing. There was only one way. So, one day the king arose, took off his crown, relinquished his scepter, laid aside his royal robes, and he took upon himself the life of a peasant. He dressed in rags, scratched out a living in the dirt, groveled for food, and dwelt in a hovel.

"He did not just take on the outward appearance of a servant, he became a servant. It was his actual life, his actual nature, his actual burden. He became as ragged as the one he loved so that she could be his forever. It was the only way. His raggedness became the very signature of his presence.

"He went and lived among the peasants, he worked with them, shared their sufferings, danced at their feasts, until finally he won the heart of the woman who had captured his."

So it is with God. Christ became one of us, lived among us, worked among us, suffered with us, danced with us— all in order to win our hearts.

Of course, no parable explains every aspect of the spiritual truth it communicates, but Kierkegaard's story illustrates an important point. When the Son of God became one of us, He demonstrated the incomprehensible love of God for us and His inexpressible grace toward us.

Our God could have commanded us by force to love Him; but that would not be love. He could have revealed Himself in all His majesty and power and glory; but then we would either submit to Him in fear or because of what He could do for us. And in that scenario, we would not relate to Him or believe that He could relate to us. He would be there in the heavens, and we would be here in our dust and rags.

But because He is an intimate God, He chose to draw near to our hearts by enduring what we do, living as we do, losing as we do, experiencing the human condition as we do. Intimacy is sharing. Intimacy is relation and we are only as connected as our commonly shared experiences. God knew that. He knew us. He knew we would only love Him if we knew He could relate to us. *This* is why Jesus. *This* is how the Creator of the universe, our Creator, chose to win our love. I cannot imagine a more romantically epic truth than this... Can you?

As we come to the close of this book, and as I come to the close of every time in my life when I have attempted to help people understand the truth of our Lord, a hopeful sense of wonder carries me into the thought that one day we will all see the whole picture, and we will gather with those that in some moment or season crossed our path here.

Then, I am forced to realize that this gathering will not include everyone. If it has not become apparent, as a child and student of the Lord, I hold a trusting reverence for the infinite wisdom of God; but as a simple man, I wish this were not the case. I wish there was a way those who had rejected God could somehow change their mind and turn to Him.

Then I am reminded that God is timeless and all knowing. As I have repeatedly stated throughout this volume, He is also just and fair, and "would rather have mercy than sacrifice." (Matthew 12:7)

Knowing these established truths about God, one can only come to the heartbreaking conclusion that, concerning some, God knows that no amount of time would suffice to see them believe.

No matter how much love I have for someone; no matter what sacrifices I might make for someone; no matter how many ways I attempt to convince them, or how much time I invest in that effort—I cannot force them to accept my love or anything I might offer them.

There is one barrier, one thing every human possesses that cannot be overcome—their own free will—their individual freedom to *choose*.

The Bible says that only God knows the heart of a person, and it says that only God knows the end from the beginning. (Jeremiah 17:10; Isaiah 46:10)

The most common response to this revelation is "Then what's the point? If God knows what we will do, then how do we have any choice?"

With this notion, we impose a restriction on God that is not there. Our free will to choose is in no way affected by the fact that God knows what that choice will be. It does, however, justify God's decision, from His knowledge of our ultimate decision, with regard to the time we may be given.

If I "TiVo" (record) a game I want to watch after work, and on my way home a friend calls and tells me the score, my knowledge of that game's outcome in no way affects the free will of those players while I'm watching. Though I know how it will play out, every individual decision is unchanged by what I know.

And true justice is such that for God to intervene (against our free will) for one of us would require His equal intervention for the rest of us. At one time and place in the history of mankind, God has done this. He has intervened for all of us at the cross of Christ.

I wish I could make this choice for you; but it would mean nothing for me to do so. It would mean nothing for God to do so.

True love respects the free will of another. In their book, *"I Don't Have Enough Faith To Be An Atheist,"* Norman Geisler and Frank Turek share a story with which I can relate all too well. I hope that you can too.

> "A young man is brought before a judge for drunk driving. When his name is announced by the bailiff, there's a gasp in the courtroom—the defendant is the judge's son! The judge hopes his son is innocent, but the evidence is irrefutable. He is guilty.

> "What can the judge do? He's caught in a dilemma between justice and love. Since his son is guilty, he deserves punishment. But the judge doesn't want to punish his son because of his great love for him.

"He reluctantly announces the sentence: 'Son, you can either pay a $5000 fine or go to jail.'

"The son looks up at the judge and says, 'But, Dad, I promise to be good from now on! I'll volunteer at soup kitchens. I'll visit the elderly. I'll even open a home to care for abused children. And I'll never do anything wrong again! Please let me go!'

"At this point, the judge asks, 'Are you still drunk? You can't do all of that. But even if you could, your future good deeds can't change the fact that you are already guilty of drunk driving.' Indeed, the judge realizes that *good works can't cancel bad works!* Perfect justice demands that his son be punished for what he has done.

"So the judge repeats, 'I'm sorry, son. As much as I'd like to allow you to go, I'm bound by the law. The punishment for this crime is $5000 or you go to jail.'

"The son pleads with his father, 'But, Dad, you know I don't have $5000. There has to be another way to avoid jail!'

"The judge stands up and takes off his robe. He walks down from his raised bench and gets down to his son's level. Standing eye to eye next to his son, he reaches into his pocket, pulls out $5000, and holds it out. The son is startled, but he understands there is only one thing he can do to be free—take the money. There's nothing else he can do. Good works or promises of good works cannot set him free. Only the acceptance of his father's free gift can save the son from certain punishment."

"God is in a similar situation to that of the judge— He's caught in a dilemma between his justice and his love. Since we've all sinned at one time in our lives, God's infinite justice demands He punish that sin. But because of his infinite love, God wants to find a way to avoid punishing us.

"What's the *only way* God can remain just, but not punish us for our sins? He must punish a sinless substitute who voluntarily takes our punishment for us (sinless because the substitute must pay for our sins, not his own; and voluntary because it would be unjust to punish the substitute against his will). Where can God find a sinless substitute? Not from sinful humanity, but only from Himself. Indeed, God *Himself* is the substitute. Just as the judge came down from his bench to save his child, God came down from heaven to save you and me from punishment. And we all deserve punishment. I do. You do."

Maybe this is your first-time hearing any of this. Maybe you've been considering these things for a while now—maybe a very long while.

One of the greatest bastions for the case for Christ was C.S. Lewis who made a couple of statements quite fitting to leave with you. "Christianity, if false, is of no importance, and, if true, of infinite importance. The one thing it cannot be is moderately important."

"A man who was merely a man and said the kind of things Jesus said would not be a great moral teacher. He would either be a lunatic—on the level with the man who says he is a poached egg—or else he would be the Devil of Hell. You must make your choice. Either this man was, and is, the Son of God: or else a madman or something worse. You can shut him up for a fool, you can spit at him and kill him as a demon; or you can fall at his feet and call him Lord and God. But let us not come with any patronizing nonsense about his being a great human teacher. He has not left that open to us. He did not intend to."

We are all hardwired to rebel. And especially against anything so seemingly invasive as Christianity. There are far easier religions from which to choose as it relates to consumption and simplicity. The problem, the inescapable reality we all know we face, is there is *one truth* which will be revealed as the *actual truth*, and if indeed Christianity—the truth of the resurrected Jesus—is *that truth*, well then, as Mr. Lewis has said, "it is of infinite importance;" indeed, *eternal* importance.

> "If Christianity was something we were making up, of course we could make it easier. But it is not. We cannot compete, in simplicity with people who are inventing religions. How could we? We are dealing with Fact. Of course, anyone can be simple if he has no facts to bother about."
> ~C.S. Lewis

Though the message of the cross can seem complicated, and the process of coming to a full theological understanding of all God has done to bring it to fruition is the task of a lifetime, the key to access the wisdom behind it, and the choice to enter a relationship with the Author of salvation could not be simpler. It is not a "leap of faith," as you may have thought, but a *step*. It is to step in God's direction, simply and sincerely.

> "He is wooing you from the jaws of distress to a spacious place *free from restriction* to the comfort of your table laden with choice food." (Job 36:16)

Sounds very much like a romantic invitation to a magnificent dinner date.

At the beginning of this book, I spoke of how it would benefit those who do not yet know God to step into that reality for a day. I wish there were some way I could take you forward in time in a life in which you had embraced God's love for you. I wish that I could pull back the curtain, open that door, and show you this amazing truth and its experience.

I wish I could show you the Creator of the universe longs for a relationship with you. This is *not a life of restrictions* that would somehow rob you of fun or excitement, but a life beautifully connected to the one Person who knows your every flaw and loves you unconditionally as a good parent loves their child—a relationship in which your complete trust in the One who holds every approaching moment in His hand, brings a peace you never dreamed possible—a relationship in which He progressively reveals Himself, who you truly are, and the purpose for which He created you.

I wish I could take you into those moments when you suddenly realize the power, favor, and wisdom that are yours in partnership with Him and the inexpressible joy and excitement it brings to know that you are an important part of God's amazing plan for eternity; to know He has made you a part of this great mystery of love.

Put all other thoughts aside for just a moment and ask yourself: *What if this is true? What if God has been in pursuit of me, calling me, drawing me aside to Himself?*

What if I finally stopped rebelling against this, and just gave Him the chance to show me?

Faith is not some secret ability; some tricky, difficult, or special thing, that only few master. It is simply saying, *Yes, ok; I will step toward you and choose to believe You will show me.*

Just say, "*Jesus if You are who You claim to be, then show me.*"

Remember, God says to you, "Call to Me, and I will answer you, and show you great and mighty things which you do not know." (Jeremiah 33:3)

If you will speak that, sincerely, I promise you (He promises you), He *will* reveal Himself to you.

"...what must I do to be saved? They replied, 'Believe in the Lord Jesus, and you will be saved...'" (Acts 16:30, 31)

I ask you; if you were to come up with a way for your children to be saved from the consequences of their rebellion, would you make it difficult, or as easy as you possibly could?

God has made it easy... It is *we* who make it hard.

"All your life an unattainable ecstasy has hovered just beyond the grasp of your consciousness. The day is coming when you will wake to find, beyond all hope, that you have attained it, or else, that it was within your reach, and you have lost it forever." C.S Lewis, *The Problem of Pain.*

Chapter Fourteen

NECESSARY EVIL?

"Try to exclude the possibility of suffering, which the order of nature and the existence of freewill involve, and you find that you have excluded life itself." ~C.S. Lewis

One of the most common objections to the existence of God is the fact there is such an incredible amount of evil in the world. If God is so good, so loving, and all powerful, why does evil exist? I am aware that I have previously addressed some of the points in this chapter. I reiterate them here, in this context, for the purpose of greater clarity, retainability, and to support the views in this, and the following final chapter. Bear with me as we dive a bit deeper, expand our purview, and pull together what we've discussed in light of the purpose of this book.

Understanding anything requires asking the right questions. One of the first questions must be: What do we mean by good? "What is *good*?" How do we know, or how are we aware, of goodness? How do we define *good*? In what context are we able to recognize *good*? Good is the act of kindness, mercy, justice, compassion, sacrifice, and empathy. But how are these things possible? Why are any of these acts necessary? Good, if it is to be defined in the human experience is, for all intents and purpose, a reaction. Evil can encompass many things, but is most easily defined by its results. Its consequences are how we are able to perceive evil. It seems, at least in our experience, that evil needs good to define itself. Would there be any need for our acts of good apart from evil?

Pain, suffering, heartache, despair, slavery (bondage), sickness, loss, and death are just some of the manifest results of evil. In most every situation, the acts of evil, which produce these consequences, in an overwhelming majority, are caused by the results or influence of a prior evil act. You've probably heard the statement, "Hurting people hurt people."

In turn, good can also be perpetuated by this same "domino effect." This dynamic can be traced back to the very beginning of human existence. Evil was "born" if you will. Both good and evil (in humanity) entered at some point and had their respective beginnings. Hold that thought to the side.

C.S. Lewis wrote, "Free will, though it makes evil possible, is also the only thing that makes possible any love or goodness or joy worth having." If love is to be experienced, it must come by choice. Forced love, as we've discussed, and all recognize, is a contradiction—an oxymoron.

Therefore, if there is to be any world in which love exists, there must exist the free will to choose against it. Remember, the Bible says that God *is* love. If this is true, then any love we may expect to possess ourselves must come from the source. If God *is* love, we can only have obtained love from God. He is not simply the reason it exists, or that it exists *in* Him, though it certainly does—He literally *is* love.

Oxygen is what we need to live. Oxygen is not the reason or cause of oxygen. It just *is* oxygen. We have it because *it is*, and not in any sense because we have chosen it. An odd analogy, but to say that we have no choice of its existence, nor the choice to go on living *without* it. The undeniable need for it is there, and it is provided. We do, however, have a choice to choose to use it or not. We could decide to place ourselves in a situation where oxygen was not available, choosing against its provision (removing it). What we cannot choose are the results of this rejection—to choose against oxygen is to cease living. We have the free will choice to continue living here on earth or not. Oxygen is an absolute necessity for life. We must continually choose to have access to it, if life is what we desire. Oxygen is obviously *good*, but we have the free will to reject it. In rejecting it, by default, we choose bad.

We would not call the necessity of oxygen unfair. We realize that it just *is*. We do not feel that oxygen is being "pushed on us," as if we feel there should be some other way to breath. We realize it for its properties, for what it is, and without it there is death. Absence of oxygen (something good) equals death (something bad). Absence of good equals bad.

As we move forward, I would like you to humor me by contemplating an extreme scenario. Imagine suddenly we were all informed that the Earth's atmosphere was quickly running out of breathable air. Let's say, for the purpose of this exercise certain environmentalists had been right, and the day had arrived in which this planet was no longer inhabitable.

Luckily, there were some very wise people who had prepared for this day, and we were all being asked to put on a spacesuit, so that we could be transported to another planet in order to survive. Since moving eight or nine billion people is a monumental endeavor, this transfer would take about twenty years to complete. You were told that as long as you kept your spacesuit on, you would be protected until it was your turn to leave. We'll come back to this.

C.S. Lewis said, "If a thing is free to be good, it is also free to be bad." We talked about how both good and evil had their respective beginnings, and I could labor the point, but I think I've shown it quite obvious, love is not love if you don't have a choice in the matter.

So, if a God, who *is* love, had created a *good* world, I suppose we would all agree by "good" we mean a world where the experience of love was possible. If Lewis's statement, which also seems fairly obvious, is true—that if we are *free to be good*, we would be *free to be bad*, then the possibility of the existence of evil would be inevitable. I mean, once you decide that love must be included, and true love only exists with choice, then there is no avoiding the fact that someone, at some point, was going to make the alternative choice for bad. It is quite interesting, and says much about us, that this temptation did not even survive the very first humans.

What if the simple truth is in order to give us the greatest possible existence, in the greatest possible experience (which we all recognize is love), there were no world, *with love*, that could escape the possibility of evil? What if all our complaining about a world with pain has really been to say nothing else but how thoroughly appalled we are to have found that God has had the audacity to introduce us to the beauty of love?

The experience of the sensation of warmth is not possible without cold. Joy is not possible without the sorrow which defines it. The inescapable truth is, we could never have intimately experienced our Creator apart from love—apart from free will—apart from the possibility of evil.

Again, an inevitable equation emerges: love = free will = the possibility of evil = the choice of evil = loss = pain = compassion = sacrifice = love. It would seem a Creator determined to introduce love (to introduce Himself to His creation) would have to be willing to embrace the possibility, and maybe the *probability*, that to reach the experience of ultimate intimacy, and a complete revelation of Himself, the possibility of evil could not be avoided. To have made us automatons would have abandoned any possibility of love. For a God whose very essence is love, one could not reasonably see this as an option.

How then might a God like this remedy such a thing? How would an all knowing, all powerful, and timeless God of love, who possesses nothing of evil, and could not coexist with a creature who does, reconcile such a dilemma?

He might create something that in a very awkward sense resembles a spacesuit—a protective covering. Perhaps He might provide a way for His beloved creatures to be sustained and eventually delivered from the polluted and hostile environment created by the choice of evil.

Perhaps His plan all along had been to show His creatures that the power of this great love would conquer evil, and bring creature and Creator together in a way that would have otherwise never happened.

Even if I had never known the story of God, I could not bring myself to believe that a Creator, who could introduce us to something so magnificent and mysterious as the wonder of love, would not also possess the passions, devotions, self-sacrifice, and most notably the honor, our experience sees us capable of through love.

One of the things God reveals as you grow closer to Him is the physical world mirrors the spiritual world.

Scientists have determined, in what is called the second law of thermodynamics, the universe is "winding down," losing energy, decaying if you will.

The truth is, there is also an increasingly toxic spiritual atmosphere surrounding us. There is a day approaching that *will* see us transported from this planet. God has provided a remedy. He has reconciled the problem of evil and all its horrid results. He has provided a "protective covering" that delivers us from the hostile environment of mankind's fateful choice. I don't imagine there would be many who would have a problem accepting the spacesuit necessary in our scenario to sustain them if our planet became so physically polluted. I think most have the sense and survival instinct to choose life.

Undoubtedly there would be those who mocked the idea of it, who ignored the warnings, and refused the special suit. Regardless of what they believed concerning the evacuation, and need for this suit, the truth would not change. Their opinions would have absolutely no effect on the reality they would indeed die without protection. Just as there were, in our scenario, very wise people who prepared and provided for us, God prepared and provided for His creation to be delivered from eternal death as well.

So, let's talk a bit about the prevailing question of pain and suffering in the world and the accusations swirling around the perceived indifference of God. As an apologist I get all kinds of questions. In the time I've been engaged in defending truth there are a number of questions of which I can be almost assured. One has to do with God's indifference to intercede in our lives to stop bad things from happening. "Why didn't God stop the murderer from pulling the trigger?"

First, we must see *what* we are actually asking God to do. Do we want God to stop all evil? What if He started with us? We all do evil on different levels. If God were to stop one evil, would He not be obligated, by integrity, to stop all evil? If God were to intervene on behalf of one approaching evil, He would then, in fairness, be bound to intervene in all. If He were to do that, we would no longer be free creatures. To interject Himself into every circumstance where evil was chosen by humans would be to remove free will altogether. His apparent answer to this, in His mercy, is to, as the Bible tells us, "Take what was meant for evil and turn it for good." The timeless ability to know perfectly how all things will play out affords an all-powerful God the means to see to it even those most horrible of events produce an ultimate good while still allowing each of us our own choices. We refer to this as the ripple effect. Tragedy is sometimes the only thing that gets our attention.

What would a world without pain and suffering actually look like? We've seen there are many things which make up the world as we know it requiring their opposite to even be recognized, defined, and exist in our reality. As discussed, *right* can only be genuinely defined as an opponent to *wrong*. Right needs wrong to define itself, experientially. Joy has no significantly measurable place in reality without pain. Hope emerges as recognizable, almost exclusively, by being forced on us by the presence of fear, despair, loss, or some adversity. No one hopes for what they already have.

Bliss, ecstasy, or any other level of pleasure is justified in our minds as such as an alternative to varying levels of discomfort resulting from loss, isolation, depression, illness, and what we see as cold, hard things. Comfort needs the companion of discomfort to exist, and a warm bed would never enter your reality without knowing a chill. Each *good* experience becomes great, wonderful, exceptional, spectacular, fantastic, and then blissful ecstasy, depending, and *only* depending, on their corelative opposites and their chronological proximity to each other as they take place within the events of our lives.

This "flatline theory," or if you like, relative experience, is an unavoidable dynamic. The necessity of highs and lows is indispensable. If there were no "down" from which to come up, and instead our experience avoided any spectrum of emotional variation, there would be no love, joy, or goodness of which to speak. Empathy, sympathy, compassion, or kindness would not be necessary apart from need.

Human society would simply interact for material, monetary purposes of business, much like ants moving robotically in a passionless, mechanical existence. The *flatline* problem reveals that we need the spectrum of an emotional humanity, with varying levels of discomfort, to produce the empathy required for compassion, sacrifice, and any experiential definition of love.

It's any easy thing to suggest that pain and suffering should be removed completely, until you understand the real-world implications of such a move. Look again at the truth in this inevitable relational formula.

(Loss = love)
Loss = pain and suffering.
Pain and suffering = compassion.
Compassion = sacrifice.
Sacrifice = love.
Loss, as strange as it may seem, equals love.

We cannot escape the fact pain and suffering are the direct results of free will. Free will is the result of a loving God seeking to give us the greatest, most fulfilling existence possible. As tempted as we are to reject it, without pain and suffering, a world that possesses the possibility of love would be impossible. Quite literally, pain and suffering are a justified result of a good and wise God. In God's wisdom, He has foreseen, then allowed, pain and suffering in order to give us the ultimate human existence. Humanity as we know it, and consequently an accurate revelation of and *relation* to the character of our Creator (and our need for Him), would not be possible in any alternate reality.

Good could never be fully defined in our conscience aside from the existence of evil. God gave us the picture of a world without evil in the Garden of Eden, a reference and presentation of His ultimate hope and will for us. He also knew, and rationally we can see, that without an experience absent that pure and innocent existence, we would never be able to appreciate it. I would suggest without the experience we now know, we could not have the reference to one day fully appreciate heaven. "You don't know what you've got till it's gone."

So, while complaining of the existence of evil, we must realize we would never know we should complain without evil. There would be no experiential comprehension of good without the presence and corelative taste of evil. Without bitter, there is no definable cognitive experience of sweet. If sweet were an isolated invariant sensation, with no spectrum that moves even a fraction toward bitter, there would be no pleasurable differentiation. Have you ever eaten anything that seemed to have no taste at all? You only know it is tasteless having known flavor. I labor the point, but without the juxtapositions provided us, without an opposing spectrum of comfort and discomfort, life would be tasteless with no flavor at all. My guess is, in a world like that, though we would have no pain, it would do very little to stop our complaining.

We only recognize evil because there is a *standard* for good. There is an innate part of us that seeks justice, urges kindness, and rejects evil because we are made in God's image and likeness. If there is a moral law, which all humans recognize, then there is a moral law Giver. We only observe a moral law in light of evil. Evil is not proof of the absence of God, it is definitive proof of His presence.

In our experiential reality, we see that pain is the greatest agent for change. In *"The Problem of Pain,"* C.S. Lewis explains the practical application of pain in the hands of our divine Parent:

> *"Pain* insists upon being attended to. God whispers to us in our pleasures, speaks in our consciences, but *shouts* in our pains. *It* is His megaphone to rouse a deaf world."

In comfort, the human tendency is complacency—to remain stagnant. The Word refers to a "river of life." (John 7:38; Revelation 22:1; Ezekiel 47:9) A river is not just coming from somewhere; it is going somewhere. Stagnant reservoirs die. The Dead Sea has an inlet, but no outlet. Humans are never more motivated to move, and to change, as when they are in pain.

My brother-in-law was a heroin addict for a significant part of his life. It is an addiction with the strength of few others, and the physical toll can be a continuous revelation. The effects of this prodigal lifestyle finally came to a head for my brother-in-law several years ago, and he was forced to think about things he had never really before considered. Like many of us, Gary hadn't given much serious thought to God. When he learned that cancer was ravaging his body, he began, for the first time in his life, to pray.

Gary called his sister (my wife) and expressed that he really didn't think he knew how to pray, and he wanted to talk to someone who knew about God. Now, one could shrug off this reaction as fear, but what really was happening was Gary reaching out for that which he knew in his heart he had always needed. Gary had never given his heart to Jesus. The truth is, aside from receiving the devastating news he had very little time to live, he may never have come to God. He could've been hit by a car or been taken out by any number of sudden accidents. He could have fallen asleep one night, never to wake up. There were likely innumerable instances throughout Gary's risky life as an addict when he could have easily died from an overdose, or in some drug related incident.

All these probable scenarios would have robbed him of the opportunity of reconciliation and eternal life with God. But God did not want that for Gary any more than He wants that for us. In His amazing grace and mercy, in a wisdom only fully known to Him, God allowed the pain Gary needed to turn him toward Jesus, and ensure he would not be lost.

Only an omniscient God knows what it will take for someone to acknowledge Him and the sin which separates them from Him. Only an omnipresent (timeless) being, who knows the end from the beginning and the hearts of those who will come to Him, and those who will not, can be trusted and justified in any circumstantial action to fulfill that end. God can stop any scheme of the devil at any time. He can, and often does, heal people of their afflictions. The question is then asked, "Why does God heal some and not others?"

Since the existence of pain, as we've seen, is a virtual prerequisite for an ultimately fulfilling human experience, as well as a revelatory tool, and since the stubbornness of the complacent soul within a certain level of comfort is humanity's propensity, God, with foreknowledge of this hindrance, will use the power of pain for eternal good. It may be, in one person's case, only in the face of death will they choose God. In another's case, the people surrounding someone who is ill may be drawn near to God through that person's miraculous healing. The bottom line is there is only One who knows without any doubt or fallibility what is precisely needed in the heart of each person for them to make the choice, in their own free will, for God.

Again, as we are with our own children, God is less interested in the vehicle necessary to bring a good outcome as He is that the desired outcome is reached. If physical discipline becomes the only thing to bring our children to a place of wisdom and understanding which will serve their success in life, we are willing, and even obligated, to utilize it. As painfully difficult as it is in the moment correction is being applied to them, we are willing, in light of promised success, to bring the benefit of that painful and motivating catalyst into their experience. Why are we so surprised when our heavenly Father utilizes the same strategy?

The relatively light affliction is employed to avoid the probability of a much more devastating one. Again, we have no problem grasping the necessity of this dynamic as it concerns us as parents, but we are somehow blinded to the same wisdom with respect to God.

The thing to remember is, as humans, we are capable of error in our execution of judgment or strategic dispersion of pain. God however is perfect to this end—able to allow with complete accuracy the amount of adversity required to see the greatest good accomplished. There is an unequivocal peace one possesses when they come to a full revelation of this—to know with absolute assurance God knows all, is all-powerful, is infallibly just, is all-merciful, is pure love, and His plans for you are good beyond what you are able to fathom. This remains true even when there seems no reasonable explanation for the pain you are enduring. To trust in God is to know no more pain than is absolutely necessary for your greatest good will ever come to you—no less—but not one fraction more.

In August of 2008 I was arrested for my fourth DWI. I was then sentenced to two years in prison and lost everything I owned—a marriage, a career, and precious, irretrievable, time with my children. After three months in county jail, I landed in Middleton Unit in Abilene Texas. The penitentiary was my reality, convict was my label, 1529041 was my number.

I had a lucrative business, owned a house where I lived with my wife and two young children, and suddenly, it was gone. That pain, that fear, that heartache, that despair was *the most* overwhelming, miserable experience of my entire life. Some of what took place while I was locked up, I will never fully share with anyone. I learned the true meaning of horror, and almost every aged line in the face of evil. In ways and in secret places, supernaturally provided for me, the Lord sanctified and transformed me.

The contrast of what I can only describe as heaven in the mist of hell, was something I never thought possible. I just want to say, if you are reading this book while incarcerated, know this: What you see around you is one thing, and undeniably it is real, but not as real as the power of our Lord and His kingdom. All you are facing, all that seems to have control of your existence right now, the authority of the state, the dynamics of the games that go on with other inmates, what's happening with your loved ones in "the world," the reality of what everything looks like concerning your case, everything; everything is subject to the grace and power of God.

Please understand this, my brother, my sister; if you will submit yourself completely to the Lord, in prayer and relentless diligence to the study of the Word, totally relinquishing all control and every circumstance to Him, you will begin to see a world *more free* than you ever were on the outside. You will experience a peace, through purpose and in the Spirit, that will actually cause an indifference to, and an acceptance of, the time that now consumes your thoughts. I know that may seem impossible, but I'm telling you, when it came my time to leave, I was saddened in many ways. Because of what God had done there, because of my true experience of the power of the kingdom, what I had first considered hell became the most wonderful place I had ever been.

Before my time was served, I felt more completely alive, full of peace, and joy, and truly the man I was created to be, than I ever imagined possible. Purpose was not only defined for me but assigned to me. The miracles God allowed me to be a part of, the lives of the men who were eternally altered, I am convinced, never could have taken place any other way.

The ability, for the first time, to understand who I truly am, and the reality of what life is all about, could have only been realized by going through that storm. Just as God had done with Noah, He hit the reset button, and started my life over. It was so much more than that though. He pulled back the curtain, removed blinders from my eyes I never knew were there, and showed me a completely different world of reality—the way He sees the world. It was, it *is*, an unexpected beauty so spectacular you want everyone to see it.

Each of us, somewhere deep within ourselves, imagines, longs for, hopes for, desperately wants to believe in, that magical place that exists only in our dreams. That is no accident. I found that place! I found it, in of all places, waiting at the end of a hall of suffering, on the other side of what seemed an insurmountable cliff of despair, and inside a pain I had never expected. It turned out I would only "find" God, and myself, at the very bottom of a cold, hard pit—broken into a million pieces. It was, and is, the most wonderful surprise of my life. As strange as it may be, I have come to understand that God's purpose for my life could have taken no other route.

In a similar way, God came to our brother, Gary. With no knowledge of Gary's addiction issues, our church administrator heard the name of one of the men in our street ministry. His unlikely name just inexplicably came to mind—Jesse. He called immediately to set up a meeting with Gary. Soon it became all too clear this was a divine appointment. It turned out Jesse was an ex-heroin addict himself—exactly from whom Gary needed to hear.

One of the most effective ways God uses the pain we endure is in the relative connection we will have with those souls with which He knows we will come in contact. There are certain people who *you* would be able to reach that I, or someone else, would not, simply because you have been where they are now. They *know* you understand their plight. They *know* that you hear them. The universal truth about people is they will not sincerely care what you have to say until they are convinced you care about what they have to say.

Empathy is the ability to experientially understand other's feelings as if we were having them ourselves, because in some way, we have shared that experience. Sympathy, though important, is the less intimate ability to take part in someone else's feelings in a caring, less relative, manner—mostly by feeling sorry about their misfortune, rather than knowing specifically how that misfortune truly feels. Sympathy says: "I can't imagine how difficult this must be for you." While empathy says: "I *do* understand, I *can* imagine, and can almost completely put myself in your shoes. I don't have to *imagine* your pain because I've been there."

Had I attempted to relate to Gary's addiction through my own experience with alcoholism, Gary may have thought he was, in some way, worse than me, or less worthy than me. Perhaps he had also struggled with alcohol and knew there were certain ugly places heroin addiction could take you that alcohol could not. This difference could cause Gary to see himself, or his transgressions, as more serious, and consequently less forgivable. Remember, Gary had little understanding of God's grace. People don't know what they don't know.

When Gary met Jesse, saw and heard how Jesus had forgiven and saved him, suddenly there was hope. Gary realized, in spite of the fact Jesse once embraced the same ugly darkness as he, God loved him, had forgiven him, and transformed his life. As we all stood there, Gary was overcome by that love himself. There is no greater privilege, no comparable experience in all of life, like watching someone changed by the love of Jesus. Less than a month later, Gary went to be with his Lord, Who, in His great and provisional wisdom, knew *what*, and *who*, it would take to change Gary's eternal destiny and bring him home.

Pain and suffering are indeed an often-difficult mystery, but, what I have learned about humanity, specifically in my role as a parent, reveals pain as a strangely wonderful, dare I say beautiful, necessity.

I am five years sober as of this writing. I am involved in prison ministry, serving the Lord as an addiction counselor, and a book author. I am married to my best friend, am financially blessed with a wonderful little place in the world, and I am continuously watching relationships in my life restored.

There is purpose in pain. Only those trained and purified by its fires will understand that. I can sincerely and humbly proclaim: I can not only see the necessity in pain, but can honestly say how very grateful I am for all it has provided me and my family.

Please understand, in no way do I mean an insensitive trivialization of the pain in people's lives. I can certainly relate to the anger and sorrow, that can accompany pain and suffering. I have had some very heated exchanges with God over that which seemed unfair and completely unreasonable to me. There is, and always will be, a part of me that wishes there were no pain. But in the same moment I have that thought, I am forced by experience, logic, and reason, to admit if given the power to remove it, I would have no better solution to replace all it provides. I have reached the inescapable conclusion: without the existence of pain, we would forfeit every beautiful facet of what it means to be human, the providential motivation to change, and any real possibility of an authentic, tangible experience with love.

I am no longer offended or confused by a world which includes pain. But the arrogance of finite beings to question an infinite God? Well, that is the much tougher problem to explain.

C.S. Lewis writes,

"...if you really get into any kind of touch with Him you will, in fact, be humble—delightfully humble, feeling the infinite relief of having for once got rid of all the silly nonsense about your own dignity, which has made you restless and unhappy all your life."

You see, God wanted to give me peace—a rest in Him that produces a powerful strength in our lives—an unobstructed focus or vision of true value, with a strong and matured wisdom, able not just to handle, but conquer anything. Knowledge that our power lies only in Him, and His purpose for us, trumps any other counterfeit satisfaction which ultimately ends in futility. A surprising realization reveals you were all along thinking too small—that the Creator of everything was seeking a partnership with you to affect eternity, and every painful circumstance had only ever been leading you toward this wonderful revelation.

We think we know what will make us happy. Like the child who elects to "continue making mud pies because he does not know what is meant by a vacation at the beach," we think too small. God wants to remove the mud pies, clean us up, and take us on the adventure of our lives, to fulfill in us the dream we never even knew was an option.

And, if pain is what it takes to move us into that dream, His wisdom will allow it.

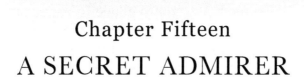

Chapter Fifteen

A SECRET ADMIRER

"...How long will you hide your face from me?"
(Psalm 13:1)

"Heard melodies are sweet, but those unheard
are sweeter." ~John Keats

The most practical obstacle challenging the belief in a Creator God of the universe is the assumption reality consists of that which can be seen with the eyes. Many concur with Michigan's state slogan "Show me!" when it comes to claims of an infinite Being Who rules it all.

My cousin, who makes no beans about his skepticism regarding the existence of God, proudly displays a quote on his Facebook page from Christopher Hitchens, one of the most well-known atheists of our time: "That which can be asserted without evidence can be dismissed without evidence." Hitchens goes on to say that "It is not for a defendant to disprove an unproven case, but rather for the claimant to produce sufficient evidence to support its allegation." What one must first notice, in what is referred to as "Hitchens' Razor," is that Hitchens assumes himself, and those like him, to be the defendant, and those who believe in God to be the claimant.

This is an assumption of presumptions. It arrogantly assumes one can automatically presume Creation is not only the less plausible idea, but indeed absurd. This presumption relies on what Hitchens believes is the absence of evidence. As J. Warner Wallace (a renowned homicide detective and Christian apologist) has cited, there are more convictions attained through circumstantial evidence, which move a jury beyond reasonable doubt, than cases where there is what is referred to as "hard" evidence. In fact, these circumstantial cases make up the vast majority of convictions.

Either the universe sprang into existence from absolutely nothing, or it was caused by something. Never, in any other place in the history of our existence, do we see something come from nothing. Everything that has ever begun to exist has *always* had a cause. The universe began to exist; therefore, the universe had a cause. This is not semantics or linguistic gymnastics. It is very simple, reasonable, and universally accepted scientific knowledge. No established scientist denies these facts. The only thing in question is the cause. Now, if there were nothing else to consider (and there most certainly is) one could not attribute the labels of "claimant" or "defendant" to either view. The question of cause has arbitrarily and independently presented itself. Christopher Hitchens could just as correctly be called the claimant as anyone who offered a view in opposition to him. However, if we were to take the reality we see in every other instance in the known universe of something beginning to exist (i.e. that it had a cause) then for Christopher to take a view of opposition to that evidence would place him much more suitably in the role of claimant.

Hitchens is bound by his own statement, *"anything that can be asserted without evidence can be dismissed without evidence." There has never been evidence that something sprang into existence from nothing.* His claim that the universe is somehow acting, in this one unique instance, differently than it does throughout the entire known universe, can much more reasonably be dismissed without evidence. His claim flies in the face of all humanity has seen and known of the origins of things; therefore, it is he that is the claimant who must provide sufficient evidence if he is to contradict all we know of our physical world.

So then, we can agree with Mr. Hitchens. It is not for a defendant to disprove an unproven case (that something can come from nothing), but rather for the claimant (Hitchens) to produce sufficient evidence to support *his* allegation (that suddenly, things that begin to exist need no cause.) In addition, DNA has been determined, by all scientific accounts, to be a language code—*information*. Information has never, in the known universe, come from anything other than intelligence. It becomes painfully and embarrassingly evident it is Mr. Hitchens who is making the absurd *claim*. His assertion that suddenly, *miraculously*, something (the universe), which all concede began to exist, in this one special instance had no cause, can indeed be dismissed without evidence. Sadly, he is now in a position to realize his error.

It is now established science—time, space, and matter all came into existence in a simultaneous instant. They call that moment, within *the Big Bang,* "Singularity." Whatever caused time, space, and matter to begin to exist, by default, must be timeless, spaceless, and immaterial.

It must also be *personal* to have chosen to create. It must have been infinitely powerful to have accomplished this. A timeless, spaceless, immaterial, personal, and infinitely powerful being... hmm, sounds very much like *God*. We are forced here to admit, at least in the science related to the beginning of the universe (and in the language code of DNA), God is anything but "hidden." I could suggest with great confidence it is more plausible that our universe, which by all accounts had a beginning, and since it is also universally accepted things which begin to exist have a cause, was so caused by an intelligent, personal, all powerful, and immaterial agent, outside time and space. This becomes much more evident by looking at the equally accepted fact the universe appears to be finely tuned, ordered, and designed.

We will look at this amazing revelation more as we move forward. But first let us seek to answer the why question. Why would a wise God, completely capable of "proving" Himself through some obvious manifestation, choose to remain virtually unseen?

Now, I know what people mean by this concept. I also know why they want God to remove *all* question of His existence. We want to be let of the hook, as it were, with regard to our responsibility to any level of faith. What is ironic is our own desire for those we have relationships with to trust us. There is what people can see of us, and what can't be seen. The part of us that is a mystery (not completely obvious) is the much greater portion of who we are. We could hear the wife proclaiming to her aloof husband, "Why won't you let me in!? Just talk to me! I feel as though you don't see me!"

We realize in every other relationship, with our fellow humans, there is what is evident and superficial, and there is what's beyond the shell. One can pick up a book like this one and have somewhat an idea, from its cover, what it may be about. We do not believe there is no real content in a book because we've yet to read it. Similarly, we would not think someone was not a real person having only observed their body. To think a person is no more than a figment of our imagination, because we do not see who they truly are, would be strange.

We see evidence for the reality of someone. They possess a physical structure that we instantly recognize: Arms, legs, torso, head, and the movement of these parts, all tell our minds this is a person. They reflect the properties we have previously witnessed and have come to know as human. In reality, we have only seen maybe 10% of the whole of that being, but much is already apparent to us. We can also recognize the existence of humans without seeing their physical bodies. I can be strolling on the beach and come across markings in the sand which, upon closer inspection, reveal the words "John loves Mary." As a result of this, though I have witnessed no other people on the beach but myself, I can confidently conclude a human had been there. If I came back to that spot on the shore every day to find a new message written in the sand, but never actually saw anyone, it would still be evident they were there.

There are many obvious physical, albeit "superficial," characteristics of God as well. They are all around us in both simple and complex representations. We reveal ourselves to others in stages, do we not? I have found that God is like this. We are very much like Him in this regard.

Let's look at the varied manifestations of God in an order of stages that He might choose to reveal Himself to a person. This order could be different depending on the person and/or circumstances. We might first meet someone in person and get to know more of their inner personality thereafter, or perhaps we might come to know their personality (over internet exchange) long before encountering them physically. So, the order of our relational revelations can be experienced in a variety of possible scenarios.

"If God is real, why doesn't He just show Himself?"

I quoted a Facebook friend in my first book who stated, "Forgive me, but I see no more reason to believe in a man in the sky, or a devil down below, than I do Santa Claus." Many are convinced the Bible is nothing more than fairytales harbored by the weak in order to make them feel better. After all, most people expect a certain amount of proof for any number of practices in their everyday lives. To be taken seriously, even as it relates to *our own existence* (who we claim to be), requires proof of identification.

In a court of law, one must present evidence of someone's wrongdoing to prove they are indeed a criminal. Until proof beyond a reasonable doubt is presented, that person cannot be identified as anything more than a normal, law abiding citizen. In fact, our entire system of life functions, to the highest degree, on proof. You must prove not only you have money, but the money you're presenting is authentic and not counterfeit. Proof is essential to a realistic and functioning society. So, when someone with faith in God says, "You just have to believe!" it's no surprise the person considering the possibility of the existence of God sees this statement as unreasonable.

Fortunately for the Christian, and those considering God, there is actually a very long list of reasonable evidence, both practical and philosophical, for the existence of an intelligent Designer, and more specifically, that this Designer *is* the God of Christianity. Let's begin with what I believe are the most significant possibilities in the philosophical implications inherent in free will as it relates to the mystery, or "hiddenness," of God. If God has indeed created us, and created us with free will to choose, then my first question would be, "Why is this the case?" Why free will rather than automatons (robots), predisposed, or programed? We've spoken at some length of free will in relation to pain and suffering. Let's continue in that thought process assuming, as we've established, without free will, love would not be possible. One must be free to choose if love is to be authentic. This answers the question "Why free will." God wanted our existence to include love.

Next question: If one were to somehow influence our choice, bringing to bear a circumstance in such a way as to intimidate us into a choice they desired, would that constitute a choice *freely* made? Example: Say I was a millionaire and was very attracted to a woman and desired her to truly fall in love with me. I might make her my wife quite easily by revealing the fact I was a millionaire, but then, her motivation could be in question. Was she marrying me because she loved me, or because of my money, power, and what I could do for her? The revelation of my wealth removes a significant amount of certainty. The only way to be sure she sincerely loved me, *for me,* would be to keep a full revelation of who I was *hidden.*

Her free will choice to join herself to me, solely born out of a love for me, would be thoroughly affected, and most probably compromised altogether, by a complete disclosure of the benefits she would gain regardless of whether love had anything to do with it. Therefore, though she might choose to believe she should join with me in marriage by her own *free* will, it may not be a choice made in response to genuinely, uncorrupted love. Indeed, it could be motivated by selfishness which, by definition, opposes and cancels love. Just as important is the fact once she has become aware of my wealth, its influence can never be omitted. She cannot unlearn or ignore it. It has entered the choice making equation and made an authentic choice of love, for its own sake, forever in question.

In the same way, one can see how a full revelation of God could affect our ability to freely, and sincerely, choose God, motivated purely by love. This might suggest by default (as is true in our marriage scenario), the possibility no future decision for love's sake alone may be possible.

What is certain, if we believe He has created us, is He would know the nature of each of us, and if authentic love is His desire, would also know perfectly how to give it the greatest possible chance to arise.

Another aspect is the way *fear* might affect our freedom to choose. This affect is much like what we have just discussed, only the motivation changes. If God were to boldly reveal Himself leaving no doubt of His existence, what do you suppose would happen? Let us imagine He descended over the White House lawn, in all His glory, accompanied by an angelic host, chariots of fire, a thunderous booming voice, and royal blue bolts of sky ripping lightening. This action would instantly stoke an immediate fear into many, especially those who had always mocked the notion of Him as nothing more than a ridiculous fairytale.

Even a more subtle appearance might have enough of an affect that those whom God had planned to draw near to Him by the means which at present He seems to employ, would likely either run, or believe in Him out of fear. Rather than the love God seeks from their choosing Him out of a gentle seduction of their hearts, a terror-fueled decision resulting from intimidation would inevitably take place. A fearful proclamation of someone's belief in us, born from forceful manipulating intimidation, is not what we want, and it cannot, in any sense, be recognized as love.

This is the relational dynamic the Lord is faced with in pursuit of you and me. As is true with human relationships, overwhelming power is never the way of love, and it removes the very possibility that a free love (the only love) can take place. God knows the human's bent toward self-preservation and the way I see it, He can either completely disclose Himself and judge us based on the default motivations that would inevitably arise (basically making our decision for us), or He could strategically display enough revelatory evidence for us to gradually succumb to the wonder inherent in such romance, so that it indeed becomes the free choice of a captured heart.

This is precisely what God has done to win us! He descended to the human level, in fact, to one of the lowest levels of society possible—that of a servant. The Apostle Paul describes Christ's efforts to relate to us on the most intimate level in his letter to the Philippians (2:5-8): "Your attitude should be the same as that of Christ Jesus: Who, being in the very nature of God, did not consider equality with God something to be grasped, but made Himself nothing, taking the very nature of a servant, being made in human likeness. And being found in appearance as a man, He humbled Himself and became obedient to death—even death on a cross!"

To say God is hidden is not true at all. Imagine the Creator of the universe humbling Himself by coming to serve, suffer, and die at the hands of the very creatures He made! The self-disclosure of God in Christ is the most amazing thing that has ever happened in the history of mankind. We should not have expected this. It is, without doubt, the most unlikely of things that could have ever taken place. And though, admittedly, so very surprising, and perhaps a million miles from the idea we might have imagined, it is *what has actually taken place—* our Creator's "oddly," unexpected, and candid revelation of Himself.

We can certainly be deceived by believing what is untrue, but we can be equally deceived by *not* believing what *is* true. Which deception is more dangerous? For you to be deceived about something that is true, and not believe it is true, when indeed it is, can be applied in a number of ways. One of the first that comes to mind is love. To believe that someone truly loves us, only to find out they do not, can be a devastating revelation. But given the opposite circumstance, that is, to believe someone does not truly love us, when they actually do, which would you rather have known? Realizing someone you thought had loved you really didn't, would hurt, but you could move on with the hope you would eventually find the one that was meant for you. But, what if you found "the one," (and their love *was* true), but walked away from them because you did not believe what was actually true. Which is the more tragic scenario?

Let's look at it another way. If somehow you knew nothing of gravity (as might be the case with a small child) and someone told you that you would die if you stepped off the edge of a high cliff, which would be the more dangerous deception; to be deceived by believing what is *untrue* (thinking that you might die even if you wouldn't) or to be deceived by not believing what *is* true (thinking you would not die when you actually would)? If you bought the notion you would fall to your death and it turned out that wasn't true, then no harm. But if you did not believe you would fall to your death, the fact it *was* true, might be the end of you.

In these examples, it would be much more dangerous or painful not to believe what was true than to be deceived by what might be untrue.

I'll give you one more to ensure we all get the point:

If I were to attempt to sail my boat from one island to the next, and I was informed of high and dangerous winds on the sea ahead of me, and I could see the other island in the distance, through a bright sunny day, with no real visual evidence of high winds, I might believe it was safe to sail. Is it more dangerous to be deceived into believing the report is true, when it is not, or to be deceived into believing it is untrue, when in reality, it is?

Love, gravity, wind—these are all things that we cannot physically see with our eyes, but what we believe or *do not* believe about them can bring devastating consequences. As we've seen, it can be, just as often as not, more dangerous when we are deceived into *not* believing what is true, than to be deceived into believing that which is untrue. This is not an argument that holds up in every circumstance, but simply food for thought, and certainly worth a contemplated assessment in questionable matters of eternal significance.

Now, let's look at morality. I believe there may be no greater "invisible" revelation of God than our universal recognition of moral law. Thought, reasoning, and what our conscious minds recognize are aspects which cannot be explained by materialism. Guilt, shame, and our reaction to horror, are as telling as any other reality known to humanity.

A man can go into a gift shop and find himself so captured by an object, in an instance when no one can see him, and in a *moment of weakness*, decide to put that object into his pocket and walk out of the store without paying. Even though no one has seen him, and he has gotten away with the theft completely, something interesting begins to take place. As he finds himself alone that evening staring at the object on his nightstand, he is inexplicably ridden with a sense of regret and self-loathing. We call that feeling "guilt." It's a very revealing notion that while telling of this kind of act we refer to it, as I just did, as "a moment of weakness." Why? Why is it a moment of weakness, or negative in any sense? Why, when the man has not been caught, when absolutely no one in the whole world has witnessed, or knows what he's done, is he faced with this pitiful view of himself, the diminishment of his self-worth—the self-imposed judgment—this demeaning, sorrowful, thought concerning his character? Why should any of this be taking place within him? You will say, "Because, even if no one else knows, he does." So—What!? If we are no more than a product of evolution, made up of chemicals and firing neurons, why would it matter? If this man came from nothing, and is headed to nothing in the end, why should this otherwise insignificant, minuscule act mean anything?

If, however, it was true we were created in the image, and likeness, of God, and if that God were the God of Christianity; a pure, good, righteous, and perfectly moral Being, and our conscience was created in the likeness of His mind, it would perfectly explain why we are put off by the immoral. It might explain why we are appalled by injustice and demand it with respect to the actions of others, and even when seeing it in ourselves.

If there is no higher standard of morality, if we are, as naturalists claim, nothing more than moist robots, the product of time and chance, where does our standard come from? If there is an unwritten, inherent, innate, and knowable moral law, there must be a moral law Giver. Why, in virtually every culture known to man, is there this universal understanding of right and wrong? Why does this principle, if we are simply made up of electronic, randomly firing pulses, transcend and permeate all of humanity? Why are we instantly distraught at the mention of a plane crash or disgusted at the thought of children being abused?

These seem obvious to us, and for good reason. Morality is so a part of the human experience we take it for granted. If we are to believe what evolution actually presents, there would be no reason to expect this ubiquitous consensus of morality to exist. We exist in a universe that has do's and don'ts; it has rules of behavior. There are things we are supposed to do and things we are not supposed to do. Every human being has this sense we are truly and really, in reality, obligated to avoid evil and do good. There is a very real sense in every human being there is an "ought"—that there is a moral imperative that comes from somewhere and it is universal. It's not just culturally shaped, even though we recognize some morality has some cultural factors in it. But, this universal "ought," this universal imperative, has to point to something bigger than humanity.

There are moral properties that are normative, and they tell us *how* we are supposed to behave. If that is the case, that they are normative, and we have moral *duties*, not just moral values, it really does cry out for a moral law Giver. Even if we don't want God to exist, there is a sense that even if we reject rules and regulations given by parents, teachers, courts, or police, when *we* are wronged in some way, we are deeply angry, and we want justice for what's been done to us, because there still remains in us a moral law we are following and sincerely believe in.

It would seem a fair deduction, if evolution, explained by Darwin as natural selection (survival of the fittest), were our reality, when society engaged in the extermination of "the weak" in order to become stronger, we should have no problem with it. But, indeed, when Germany, possibly the most civilized, educated country on the planet took this applied view in the Holocaust, the collective conscience of the rest of the world said, "No—it's wrong!" There is no way we can conclude the Holocaust was wrong if we are cultural relativists—if we believe morals come from our own cultural societies. But as we know, as was shown in the *Nuremberg Trials*, what they did was wrong, and we were willing to say that.

If there is no objective moral law, then each individual is left to what they feel, and no one else has the right to judge them. If Stalin decides the key to his survival is to kill millions of people and there is no objective good, no standard by which to definitively say he's wrong in that decision, then it is only your opinion that it is. If morality is subjective, his decision, and act of murder, based on his opinion, is as valid as anyone's.

C.S. Lewis in *The Abolition of Man* looked at all the diverse cultures and said, "there are basic moral impulses...that they agree on basic morality." But how do you explain that basic morality? Christians or others may, in some way, say God has "written it on our hearts," but the question is not necessarily how we know it. The question is why is altruism, or caring for another, a good thing? Who said? If your argument is "That it *just* is," I would suggest that sounds very much like the argument atheists criticize when it comes to some Christian's assertions of God.

To say we are just evolved altruistically (somehow inherently good) is to steal the standard of goodness from God's universe to try to make your worldview work. If one is to stand on their belief (faith) that there is no God, they must explain from where their standard for good or evil comes. If there is no objective, authoritative, moral standard beyond us, then atheism doesn't work—not if in any sense you recognize there is a universal morality that is innately known. To say being kind to others is ingrained in our behaviors is only to say *how* we know it, not from where it comes. The ultimate question here is "Why?" Why is it *right* to love and *wrong* to murder?

When we sought at Nuremburg to hold Nazis accountable, they said, "We were just obeying our government."

But, we said, "No! You had a higher obligation to obey "the good" (your conscience), *your conscious knowledge of the standard—the known universal standard of good.*

The Nazis were tried and held responsible to what is intrinsically known—a *universally assumed objective standard.* Their actions were subject, regardless of their national duty, to an objective moral law that governs humanity. Not only that, there was such solid recognition of the fact this standard resides in each of us, their very lives would be required in trade for breaking the moral law. Solely on the undeniable solidity of this notion they were found guilty of their failure to uphold it. One cannot import moral terms such as honor, kindness, and good, into an atheist system that has no way to ground these moral terms. If we are nothing more than chemical impulses, no standard could be seen as just.

Just as is the case when we meet a young man or woman with good manners and respect for people, we assume they were raised by good people, we can assume the truth there is a God, no longer hidden, who instilled in His creation a standard of morality, principled parameters, and a sense of justice that would not simply have arrived by time and chance. A moral law, innately understood by all, implies a moral law Giver.

What is most interesting is though it is in our nature to be selfish, we instantly recognize the nature of selfishness to be in error. This makes absolutely no sense unless there exists a higher standard than ourselves. God is powerfully revealed in the fact we hold all humans to this standard, unequivocally. We rightfully acknowledge simply being human requires one to be held accountable to that standard which *all of humanity* has been divinely provided. There is no other respect in which all humans are held responsible, across the board, than that of expected common decency. We so take this expectation, this assumption, for granted we miss all that it seeks to reveal to us—that there is no clearer display of the evidence of God than *within* us.

I can tell you this, in my own experience: When I have called for Him, He has answered. When I searched for Him with all my heart, I found Him. If there had not been a vacuum in which He was "absent," or my attempt to fill it by illegitimate means, or the tormenting repercussions of those futile efforts, I might have never sought Him, never found Him.

The truth is, apart from His hiddenness, there could have been nothing to miss, no opportunity to recognize His absence, no continued aching search for that which I always sensed must await me. There was but a scent that blew in on the wind of wonder, a kind of mysterious momentum that seemed to guide, balance, call, and look forward to some great expectation, teased by dissatisfaction in every counterfeit offer of love. It was as if I were in search of a unique place I had once visited, and every drab little town along the way was a disappointment. Yes, it was hidden. I wasn't completely sure what *it* was, but I always knew instantly what it *was not*.

> "Remember this, had any other condition been better for you than the one in which you are, divine love would have put you there."
> ~Charles Spurgeon

What is most interesting, and really the whole of what I'd like people to come away with, are the countless ways, subtle and obvious, God has chosen to reveal Himself and allow us to freely come to our own conclusions.

"Little science takes you away from God, but more of it takes you to Him." ~Louis Pasteur

In my earlier refutation of Mr. Hitchens' lacking assertions, I spoke briefly about two things: the beginning of the universe and the biological world (DNA). The scope of this book prevents a thorough dive into the science available. I would refer you to the simply mind-blowing facts pertinent to these subjects presented by the likes of J.P. Gills M.D.~ *Darwin Under the Microscope*, Michael Behe~ *Darwin's Black Box*, Norman Giesler, and Frank Turek~ *I Don't Have Enough Faith to be an Atheist*, Stephen C. Meyer~ *Darwin's Doubt* and *Return of the God Hypothesis*, and Lee Strobel's works, including *The Case for a Creator*. I could cite many more comparable writings but find these most palatable for the layman.

Here we are simply attempting a conclusion as it may relate to whether God's "hiddenness" is a reasonable notion, and where it may seem it to be, what might be the motivation.

I would like to suggest that we have a "secret Admirer," though it may surprise you how truly bold and transparent He is. As previously mentioned, it has been determined by leading astrophysicists our universe is in a state of accelerating expansion, and subsequently, finite, and winding down. Or, if you like, moving toward an end. For much of history the universe was thought to be eternal, stagnant, somehow stationary, or fixed in place.

Einstein's *Theory of Relativity* revealed, or rather triggered, a revelation that stunned the scientific community. Leading experts realized since the universe was not only expanding, but accelerating its expansion, it could be rewound back to a beginning. I cannot overstate how revolutionary this discovery was. It was literally on scale with the discovery of fire, and the fact the earth is round. Even greater really, because neither of those discoveries held the divine implications inherent in a beginning of everything. What amounted to a basic reverse engineering of

the universe, taken back to the "beginning of the beginning," these experts concluded there was a point at which
time, space, and matter *instantly*, and *simultaneously*,
exploded, or sprang into existence. Again, that moment,
starting smaller than the sharp end of a pin, was labeled
Singularity.

Before that point there was *nothing*. By nothing, they
mean *absolutely* nothing. No time, no space, no matter, in
any possibly conceived or imagined way, whatsoever. The
complete absence of *anything* at all. Nothing, *literally*.

As we have seen and can observe, *all* things that have
ever begun to exist in the history of the known world,
in *every* experience mankind has ever encountered or
recorded, had a cause which facilitated the beginning of
a thing, *period*. This is not speculation. In fact, it may be
in the top three most established facts *ever*. Things do not
simply pop into existence, and if they did, logic dictates
this would be our consistent experience.

This is as certain as the fact everything that goes up
(absent any influential force) *will* come down. Cause, in
relation to the beginning of things, is as certain as gravity.
No sane person argues this. This revelation completely
disrupted the world view of humanity, especially those
who had disregarded the notion of God. The expert's
explanation of this discovery? They have none. Ask any
honest astrophysicist and they will tell you this.

Since everything which begins to exist *unquestionably*
has a cause, and since the universe (time, space, matter)
unquestionably began to exist, there was, *unquestionably*, a cause. Whatever the cause, it *unquestionably* was
not made of time, space, or matter, since, *unquestionably*,
these things did not yet exist.

Something can never come from nothing, but this
is precisely what leading experts claim has happened.
Without question, you have one choice. Either *nothing*

caused something (nonsense), or *something* (outside of time, space, and matter) caused something. That is it! There are no other options.

If I were to send a secret love letter to someone who didn't know me (weird, I know), choosing not to identify myself, or write a return address, what might that person conclude? I suppose they could believe the letter simply appeared, out of thin air, and no one actually wrote it or sent it. Or, though they had no way of knowing who sent it, they could still come to the conclusion someone did. Both of these options are available to one's mind, but one is much more probable. Every other time this person ever received a letter, there had always been someone who sent it. It is certainly *possible* this *one* occurrence is the exception, but what are the odds that it is? We do not ever even consider possibilities like this, because they have never been our experience.

Now let's look at a situation in which our experience, and reality, changed through technology. This is the nature of science. The most predictable dynamic of science is the fact it is so unpredictable. The one thing that never changes in science is it is *constantly* changing. With this in mind, Charles Darwin devoted an entire chapter to reasons that would disqualify his *theory*.

> Darwin wrote: "If it could be demonstrated that any complex organ existed which could not possibly have been formed by *numerous, successive, slight modifications, my theory would absolutely break down.* But I can find no such case." (Charles Darwin~ *The Origin of Species*, 1859)

In his defense, Darwin could not see into the cell, and might have assumed there would be nothing more to it.

He could "find no such case," but somewhat recently, we have. Michael Behe, in Darwin's Black Box, presents his discovery of what he calls "*Irreducible Complexity.*" Behe was able to prove from his discovery that, like a mouse-trap, to remove any one part of the cell mechanism is to render it completely unfunctional. You can read his findings in depth, but what Darwin himself said would "absolutely break down his theory," is exactly what Behe has found. We now live in a world where it is a fact simultaneous mutations (the opposite of "numerous, successive, slight modifications"), would have to take place in order for Darwin's theory of evolution to be valid—they do not. Darwin stated if this were the case, *then he had been wrong.*

> "In the abstract it might be tempting to imagine that irreducible complexity simply requires multiple simultaneous mutations—that evolution might be far chancier than we thought, but still possible. Such an appeal to *brute luck* can never be refuted... Luck is *metaphysical speculation* (faith); scientific explanations invoke causes." ~ Michael Behe, *Darwin's Black Box: The Biochemical Challenge to Evolution.* (parenthetical insert mine)

To paraphrase, Behe is saying, 'You are no longer doing science, but engaging in blind faith, to imagine, against all odds and nature, this might be true.' Listen now to Behe's conclusion about how naturally and common this conclusion is reached:

> "The conclusion of intelligent design flows naturally from the data itself—not from sacred books or sectarian beliefs. *Inferring that*

biochemical systems were designed by an intelligent agent is a humdrum process that *requires no new principles of logic, or science.* It comes simply from the hard work that biochemistry has done over the past forty years, *combined with consideration of the way in which we reach conclusions of design every day."*

Behe finally states ID (Intelligent design) is something that is settled as such in our minds in the things we see around us in everyday life. For example, when you come upon a wristwatch in the desert, you instantly recognize design, instead of some absurd notion that the sand and wind had created it over time.

Einstein once said, "The more I study science, the more I believe in God."

What our *Secret Admirer* is doing is amazing! He has made it so He can be recognized, little by little, not in what can be described as subtle, or ambiguous, either— but in undeniably evidential displays which shock, and spark giddy wonder that He had, all along, been just under our noses.

This is the playfully intricate game of lovers. If one cannot see this, they know little or nothing of the brilliant art of true romance. God uses in this moment in history, as He has all along the way, a man like Michael Behe, a man of science, to completely undermine His romantic rival through unparalleled wisdom possessed only by a Master Maker.

Check this out:

"The most essential prediction of Darwinism is that, given an astronomical number of chances, unintelligent processes can make seemingly-designed systems, ones of the complexity of those found in the cell. ID (Intelligent Design) specifically denies this, predicting that in the absence of intelligent input no such systems would develop. So, Darwinism and ID make clear, opposite predictions of what we should find when we examine genetic results from a stupendous number of organisms that are under relentless pressure from natural selection. *This is a stringent test. The results: 1) Darwinism's prediction is falsified; 2) Design's prediction is confirmed.*"

It should be noted even scientists, hostile toward Behe's discoveries, have no alternate or reasonably coherent answer for them. Many shamelessly move the goal posts. Chalk up another score for the "nice guy."

As is the case in human relationships, for some, no amount of shocking display, revelatory fact, or romantic gesture, will be enough to win one's obstinate heart. In many instances the "hard to get" tactic of subtle seduction wins the day, but there will always be those who cannot see past their own narcissistic and impenetrable wall of self. One thing is certain, at least in my experience with women, brute force is the surest road to rejection. No woman with any self-respect is ever won through merely heaving ourselves upon them. It is much more the fortuitous approach which allows things to "fall into place," respecting a woman's liberty to see herself in control of the outcome, that is most effective.

Mystery is the key to the lover's heart—the chance to wonder of what might escape them. A woman is never surer of anything than when rejecting what is being forced upon her. Nor is she more curious, and enticed, than by that which she suspects may be lost as an option.

"The most intense joy lies not in having, but in the desire... The delight that never fades, the bliss that is eternal, is only yours when what you most desire is just out of reach." C.S. Lewis, *Surprised by Joy*.

Is God playing games? Whether we admit it or not, in some sense, life is a game. Relationships are the most common and complicated game of all. Many things in this life can be regulated or navigated with logic—love, and the complexities of the human heart, are not among them. As we know, romance is really much more about attention to the smaller things, than grandiose gestures.

If I have learned anything through decades of intimate relationships, and the genesis of love, it must be that subtleties, surprise, and mystery, are vital. Some men never learn the intricacies of women. Many give up the effort early in life with the idea it is a "fool's errand." But women have always fascinated me. Finding out what makes them tick is one thing; learning through subtle displays, careful attention, and sustaining the *unknown*, or mystery, that I could play a part in the final outcome was a surprisingly wonderful revelation. It is just how we are, who we are, how He made us. It should be no surprise, having been created in His likeness, that He would take the same tactful, and exemplary approach of mystery in pursuit of us.

He reveals Himself in the cosmos, weaving His presence into the truth of our magnificent heavens. He shows up under the microscope to say yes, I AM there too. He refuses to let us forget Him as we recognize His undeniably familiar reflection within the very nature and conscience of humanity. It may be, surrounded by miracles, they have become common place to us, and our love affair with His wonder has waxed cold. Our reality is no less miraculous having abandoned our childlike amazement or taken it for granted. The woman is no less beautiful, nor her husband any less true, when time has weathered their memories. We don't fall out of love; we fall out of romance. Does our Lord know something about human relationship we don't? I think there's little doubt of that. Could the mystery He sustains be one of the wisest, and most strategic, things about Him? If mystery is the key to romance, and the Wedding Day has not yet arrived, then I would suggest God is only "playing it" as any wise man in love would.

I grew up with a song I heard just about the time I was learning this relational key. Maybe you remember it:

> *"Just hold on loosely, but don't let go.*
> *If you cling too tightly, you're gonna lose control.*
> *Your baby needs someone to believe in,*
> *And a whole lot of space to breath in."*

What if pure motives were the requirement for our faith in Jesus? What if those motives were precisely what we will be judged on? What if a full, indisputable revelation of God would corrupt those motives? What if the very thing we all think we want, to know, unequivocally, that God is real, was the surest way to usurp the possibility of a genuine motive, and remove all ability we might possess to make any reasonably unselfish decision to love God? What if a full revelation of God removed the possibility we could freely choose Him?

What if the grace of God were such that He would remain enough of a mystery so as to preserve pure motives within our liberties which would otherwise be compromised—once again, saving us from ourselves.

Remember the rich and powerful millionaire previously mentioned? What if he so loved the object of his affection that, knowing only true love can be sustained, and with the desire to give his beloved the best life, he withheld *all* that he was so their union would be authentic and uncorrupted? If she were willing to take him only for what she knew of him, and endure the scoffing of those who, in their own ignorance, suggested she might do better; if she had truly loved him for his own sake, their could be no question, once her ultimate reward had been revealed, that her love was, indeed, real. If, on the other hand, there had been no mystery, and she had fully known all other benefits apart from love alone, she may never have had the opportunity to enjoy true love, or the hidden perks.

You see, the grace, *within the mystery*, was only for the beloved's good. The mystery then becomes a completely selfless act of providence.

Jesus said, "Wisdom is justified by Her deeds." (Matthew 11:19) We can present our questions concerning the wisdom of God, but we must, with humble understanding, do so holding a fraction of the big picture not only bereft of that which is to come (the justifying deeds of wisdom), but even of that which is in ourselves, of ourselves, who we are—the complex outworking of our motivational influences. God looks on the heart of man, and though we've had millennia to consider it, we have failed miserably in our efforts to understand that heart.

We are naïve children still stuck in the struggle to comprehend love—to overcome selfishness—to eradicate pride—to reach any significant level of maturity. Relatively, as a society and as individuals, we are but emotional and social infants trapped inside a repetitive cycle of unimpressive growth, if not total stagnation. Our nature is perpetually in a state of need which cannot be satisfied. No matter what period of the human existence one may visit, we find this to be the truest, most unquestionable thing about ourselves. Any objection of this observation only serves to validate it.

The consistent futility within the rebel heart of mankind is the one over-arching reality for which we find no legitimate rebuke. It is also the greatest evidence pointing to an ultimate good and infinite wisdom. The fact we are able to recognize there is a summit or apex of maturity we cannot reach—that we acknowledge wrong and our inability to overcome it within ourselves—that selfishness is an evil and abhorrent trait from which we cannot naturally escape, but desperately long to, reveals a source that must be outside us.

This ancient dynamic leaves us, whether admitted or not, in search of that source. What if the *mystery* of God, the unknown, His *hiddenness*, His subtle invitation to a secret place, is His most strategically brilliant and providential, attribute?

As is often the case in this life, things are not always what they seem. What may seem on the surface illogical, an aggravation, or even unfair, could be the very essence of what is required for love's success, and perhaps, the only way to romance the rebel heart.

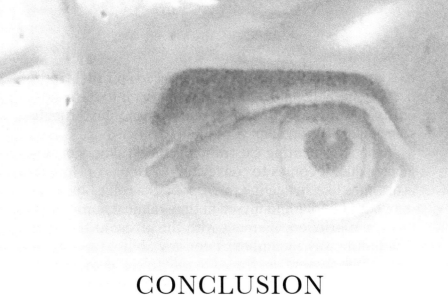

CONCLUSION

"Because man is born a rebel, he is unaware that he is one. His constant assertion of self, as far as he thinks of it at all, appears to him a perfectly normal thing. He is willing to share himself, sometimes even to sacrifice himself, for a desired end, but never to dethrone himself. No matter how far down the scale of social acceptance he may slide, he is still, in his own eyes, a king on a throne, and no one, not even God, can take that throne from him."
~A.W. Tozer

Christian writers are incessantly bound with the determination, indeed the obsession, to capture the sacred thoughts God shares with us, condense them, and corral a blazing inferno into language and onto the page—to funnel a vast sea into a linguistic river from which others can drink. "Good writing is clear thinking made visible." It often feels as though one is roping the wind or attempting to trap water with a net. With respect to spiritual truth, it's doubly challenging. Plunging your fist into the sands of Divine truth, all you wish to give seems to slip through your fingers as you open your hand to others.

Such a tormenting frustration is the weakness of language when it comes to conveying the things of God. It is at times like struggling to describe the color blue to a man born blind. I find myself at times almost humiliated by even a brief engagement with the arrogant thought it is in any way incumbent upon my ability to do this. Fortunately, we are not forced to rely solely on ourselves, and my prayer is always that God take my weak and finite efforts in faith and do, in the hearts of those who may take the time to hear me, what only He can.

If there was but one thing I was commissioned to make clear, one true "idea" which survived the sifter; If there was one simple sentence I could present to all humans and if everything I ever wanted to say hung on those few words, it would be nothing I, or any theologian, apologist, or evangelist, has ever said. If one could grasp the entire ocean of the Word of God in his hand and open it to let all run out but a few drops in the center of their palm, they would need only to have one drop survive the transfer and land in the heart of another.

If the truth of this one drop could be fully comprehended, and completely taken into the heart, for all it is, *and all it is not*, there would be no need for anything more. If we had nothing but this one statement of Jesus, it would be enough.

> "For God so loved the world that He gave His only begotten Son, that whosoever believes in Him shall not perish but have everlasting life."
> (John 3:16)

He came for *you...*

If you will simply, but diligently, do all you can within your capabilities to attempt to understand this truth, the God of all creation will continually, exponentially, reveal the greatest mystery of all time—Himself.

Our nature is to rebel. The nature we inherited from the fall of the first man and woman has caused this bent, this propensity toward rebellion. The nature we left in Eden haunts us. It calls us. It convicts us within our hearts to return to the connection we once had with God.

Isn't it interesting we all seem pulled, compelled to find that missing someone? We have even given it a name—our "soulmate." Might I suggest we *all do* have a soulmate, that Person who we are all meant to find, who we are all innately in search of, drawn to, or drawn by. He is our Creator and first love. His name is Jesus. And please, get this; as fantastic as it sounds, there is a jealous angel, with significant power, on a mission to prevent your discovery of the truth of this mystery. He, too, seeks to be your "soulmate."

There is no lie he will not tell, no scheme he will not employ, to intercept your realization of God's love for you. Every moment you come close to peering behind the curtain, he will distract you, prick your thoughts of dissent, pull your strings of rebellion, dangle the attractive temptation, bribe you with the inauthentic, trick you with the counterfeit, offer up the candy of compromise, coerce you with what it might cost you, con you with the pride of his own demise, and laugh with you at the notion of absolute truth. He will call us all fools in order to see us become one.

"Misery loves company," and there is none so bent on your miserable company as the enemy of your soul.

There will come a day, a moment, when the truth of this world and your existence will be revealed, a moment in which you will either find yourself a friend of God, or a fool for Satan. That moment is on its way to you now. Nothing can prevent it, there is no escaping it, and it could arrive this very day.

On that day, you will find yourself either in the embrace of deceptive rebellion or Divine romance. All of history has been about this one unavoidable choice within each human heart. Of all the mysteries throughout the ages, this is the one that matters, my friend. Your choice concerning this one Truth, in this very moment, will have infinite repercussions.

Each of us will stand, by our own choice, as the faithful Bride of Christ, or a harlot of the devil. The clock is winding down, the midnight hour approaches, and your God is making every effort to draw you aside to Himself— to seduce you with the truth of His love.

He knocks on the door of your heart, holding ever-lasting life in His hands. Will you continue in the rebellion of a dark prince, or choose the love of your devoted King?

May God bless you with eyes to see and ears to hear. In the name of Jesus, I ask. Amen.
Sincerely,
Patch

A DANGER

(Final Thoughts)

> *"And if there is any glory, any praise resulting from the work we achieve, let us be careful to lay it all at the Redeemer's feet." ~Charles Spurgeon*

I wrote, in the preface of this book, about the responsibility to "get right" the mysteries of God. That bringing truth, teaching it, should be less dependent on our own abilities than on our time spent in the presence of Truth.

What I have somewhat recently found, as a subtle danger, can easily put us at risk of error, because it can facilitate it. I must admit my ambition had landed me "knee deep" in, and previously unaware of, a parallel devotion. People have a propensity to become enamored with things—with what is given rather than the giver Himself.

Our danger as scholars or students of the Word presents a temptation to fall into a romance with knowledge itself rather than the Giver of knowledge. C.S. Lewis put it so well in what we now know as *"The Weight of Glory."* I read right past the point, right past the page and onto the next, before noticing. This is not an easy thing with Lewis. Even the "speed reader" will find himself in front of "roadblocks" (the depth of his reflections and use of language) time and again while reading Lewis. He forces even the most accomplished intellect to read over again his reasoning, like that tough piece of meat that must be thoroughly chewed. It may begin that way but soon you find yourself pausing to savor the thought as the finest cuisine. Lewis stirs one's mind to push them much farther than his own musings, and into their own.

Do you see what I'm doing here? We can become enamored most, in some moments, with reason, with language, with knowledge and its beauty, with what *we* may *know.*

Listen to this:

> "The intellectual life is not the only road to God, nor the safest, but we find it to be a road, and it may be the appointed road for us. Of course, it will be so *only so long as we keep the impulse pure and disinterested.* That is the great difficulty. As the author of *Theologia Germanica* says, 'We may come to love knowledge—*our* knowing—more than the thing known: to delight not in the exercise of our talents but in the fact that they are *ours,* or even in the reputation they bring us. Every success in the scholar's life increases this danger. If it becomes irresistible, he must give up his scholarly work. The time for plucking out the right eye has arrived.'" ~C.S. Lewis

It was, in fact, this quote which stopped me in my tracks and caused me to abandon part of what I had previously prepared to leave with you. Because we need to understand the principle when, at any moment, we begin to believe we can do anything of value apart from Jesus, we are subject to failure, which always comes with pride.

Rebellion takes on many different forms—not least of all our fascination with accomplishment. Suddenly, while writing this book, I noticed myself so caught up in its production that for several days I had been sprinting along in my own power, which was quickly dissipating.

Pride and lust are at the root of rebellion. How crafty is our enemy and deceitful are our hearts to find, even in service to God, we may fool ourselves—to embrace the work of the Lord to the exclusion of, or indifference to, the Lord of the work. This is the perpetual nature of the Christian life—to find time and again we have "stepped in it"—to suddenly have our eyes opened, our hearts convicted, and even that which we had been so sure of, rebuked as error.

The Apostle Paul was given a thorn, a painful messenger of humility, to keep him from this danger. *Self* is so woven into our nature as humans it becomes the chief adversary. Our earthly battle is little more than a rebellion against the rebel within us.

In Christian circles, so much time is given to the attack of outside forces coming against the kingdom—the evil that surrounds us in this secular world. When we really need look no further for our greatest obstacle, our most capable foe, than our very own soul, and its selfish passions. Indeed, this battle, above all others, is the most significant and persistent challenge we face.

As apologists, we hold the words of Christ to "love the Lord with all your *mind*" as a staple or creed of the work we do to defend our faith with reason. Paul admonished us to "Always be prepared to give an answer to everyone who asks you to give a reason for the hope that is in you."

It seems, since Christ is the Truth, that we, as I've been saying, are seduced by Truth.

The call to love the Lord with all our minds is significant and an often neglected, if not marginalized catalyst in the efforts of evangelism. Anti-intellectualism has caused great damage to the church and was not the way of the fathers of our faith. We must be careful, however, to remember Christ and truth cannot be separated—never to be swayed to the worship of knowledge itself. It may seem trivial, but there are few dangers more lethal than our very own thoughts of success, even, and perhaps especially, when succeeding for God.

For one to be so captured by the *grasping* of the mystery, in and *strictly* of itself, and to engage in an unproportionate recognition of the legitimacy of our possession of knowledge becomes—and quite often *surprisingly* becomes—idolatry.

When asked once if he were ever aware of the fact, regardless of his intentions, he was "winning worship" from his books, C.S. Lewis replied, in a low, still voice, and with the deepest and most complete humility, "One cannot be too careful *not* to think of it."

We are no more than a pond reflecting those rising mountain peaks—a clay pot formed to share the waters of God's wisdom with the thirsty—a pipeline through which truth is passed. It is not ours, and no matter how far we may think we have come, we can no more claim a single drop as our own construct, assisted by our own intellect, than to believe we can in any way manage our next breath.

Though men are plagued with their flawed notions, no such flaw inhabits, or proceeds from, God. Our inabilities, along with our perceived abilities to convey His heart, only serve as a reminder of our desperate need of His personal instruction. How fortunate we are each provided this wonderful blessing: "You will seek Me and find Me when you seek Me with all of your heart... I will be found by you, Declares the LORD." (Jeremiah 29:13,14)

We come to the knowledge of Christ, but it is not merely that knowledge that ultimately saves us. One can believe *that* Christ exists, and still not believe *in* Him. It is only in our weakness that His strength is perfected—only when we surrender to the God of the mystery and understand, each day, that this mystery is ever-widening—a race which may never finish, a vast ocean filled with never-ending treasures, yet to be discovered. Paul described it, himself, and everyone who would embark on this privileged journey: "Though I am least deserving of all God's people, He graciously gave me the privilege of telling the Gentiles (those who don't know) about the endless treasures available to them in Christ." (Ephesians 3:8 NLT)

"In Christ," you see, these treasures can only be ours when we are His. He *is* the Treasure. He *is* the us we were created to be. To rebel against Christ is to reject our very truest selves.

To become so enamored with the beauty and construct of the "bridge"—its structure, its solidity—and yet, while busily engaged in pointing to, explaining, and helping others cross over it, we ourselves fail to enjoy the fruit of its purpose—our own indispensable intimacy with God—we forfeit power. We can inadvertently ensure that our witness lacks a beauty which is far more attractive to souls than the certainty of evidential knowledge or reason. There is no greater power to convince, to draw, to capture the hearts of people, than personal intimacy with God Himself.

God has said, "Get knowledge, and in all your getting, get understanding." (Proverbs 4:7) I used to think (we are tempted to think) this means no more than understanding the knowledge we have gained, and indeed, in some respect it does. But the end of that understanding,

the true knowing, leaves for the moment language, for-
mulas, facts and evidence, and every practical reasoning
of logic, to discover the amazing revelation we can only
possess in the personal, intimate experience of the very
presence of God.

This is the "entering in." *This* has been the point of the
whole matter, all along—to draw near—to slip the bonds
of simply reading our Lover's letters and all the wisdom
they present—to meet Him—to surrender to the desire
of the Father to draw us aside to Himself, and to share
in His great love for us, and then take the power of that
love to others.

I hope you will continuously remember, with me,
this is the apex of the oracles of God, the summit of the
mountain of true faith, and the heart of the otherwise
unsearchable brilliance of the gospel—to come back to
the simplicity of its foundational essence with which He
first created us—Love.

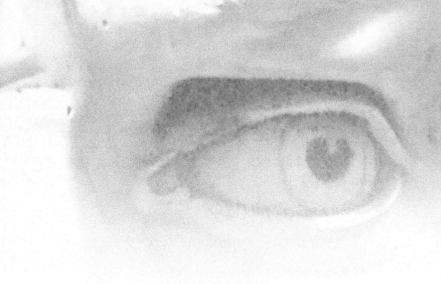

NOTES

Pg. v- C.H. Spurgeon~ *"All of Grace" (1886)*

Pg. xi- C.S. Lewis~ *"The Problem of Pain" (1940)*

Pg. 1- *Edmond de Goncourt (1822-1896)*

Pg. 2- *Soren Kierkegaard; Danish philosopher (1813-1855)*

Pg. 3- *"Chitty Chitty Bang Bang" (1968) Ian Flemming/United Artists*

Pg. 3- *Leonardo de Vinci, or John H. Secondari (1965 educational film "I, Leonardo de Vinci")*

Pg. 11- *Gregory Koukl~ "Tactics" (10th Anniversary Edition) pg. 112*

Pg. 12- *"Tough Questions" sermon series~ Dr. Jeff Wickwire*

Pg. 18- James Russell Lowell- U.S. Diplomat, essayist, poet (1819-1891)

Pg. 33- Criss Jami- philosopher (A-Z Quotes)

Pg. 46- Haile Selassie- cited from address in Adis Ababa (1963)

Pg. 48- John Stuart Mill (1867)

Pg. 52- Patch Spears~ "Anthology" (2020)

Pg. 61- Maya Angelou (Brainyquote.com)

Pg. 65- Columbia International University website

Pg. 71- Gaylord Nelson- Co-founder of Earth Day, former State Senator, Governor, and U.S. Senator-Wisconsin.

Pg. 84- Edwin Louis Cole (Brainyquote.com)

Pg. 99- John Keats (Letters)

Pg. 113- Quentin Crisp- English writer (1908-1999)

Pg. 124- C.S. Lewis~ "Mere Christianity" (1952)

Pg. 137- Robert Morris Ministries- sermon series

Pg. 140- Charles Kingsley (1819-1875)

Pg. 152- Albert Camus- French philosopher (1913-1960)

Pg. 154- David Jeremiah~ "The Book of Signs" (Cornelius Plantinga Jr.)

Pg. 155- Cornelius Plantinga Jr.- American Theologian~ "Not the Way It's Supposed To Be"

Pg. 159-Albert Einstein~ "Physics & Reality" (1936); "The World As I See It" (1932)

Pg. 168- Aldous Huxley- English writer; philosopher (1894-1963)

Pg. 168- Robert Morris Ministries

Pg. 172- C.S. Lewis~ "Mere Christianity" (1952)

Pg. 172- David Jeremiah-sermon series;TBN (Soren Kierkegaard~ "The King and The Maiden")

Pg. 177- Norman Geisler, Frank Turek~ "I Don't Have Enough Faith To Be An Atheist"

Pg. 179- C.S. Lewis~ "Mere Christianity" (1952)

Pg. 180- C.S. Lewis~ "The Problem of Pain" (1940)

Pg. 183- C.S. Lewis~ "The Problem of Pain" (1940)

Pg. 184- C.S. Lewis~ "The Case for Christianity" (1943)

Pg. 186- C.S. Lewis~ "Mere Christianity" (1952)

Pg. 192- C.S. Lewis~ "The Problem of Pain" (1940)

Pg. 199- C.S. Lewis~ "Mere Christianity" (1952)

Pg. 201- John Keats- English poet (1795-1821)

Pg. 201- Christopher Hitchens~ "God Is Not Great: How Religion Poisons Everything" (2007)

Pg. 214- C.S. Lewis~ "The Abolition of Man" (1943)

Pg. 216- Charles H. Spurgeon- English Baptist Preacher (1834-1892)

Pg. 219- Charles Darwin-naturalist (1809-1882)

Pg. 220- Michael Behe~ "Darwin's Black Box: The Biochemical Challenge to Evolution" (1996)

Pg. 220- Michael Behe~ "Darwin's Black Box" (1996)

Pg. 223- C.S. Lewis~ "Surprised by Joy" (1955)

Pg. 224- 38 Special- rock band~ "Hold on Loosely"- Warner Chappell Music Inc. (1981)

Pg. 227- A.W. Tozer (1897-1963)~ "The Knowledge of the Holy" (1961)

Pg. 231- C.H. Spurgeon (1834-1892)

Pg. 232- C.S. Lewis~ "The Weight of Glory" (1941)- (Theologia Germanica; 14th Century anonymous author)

OTHER BOOKS BY PATCH SPEARS

"THE CAPTAIN'S PEN"

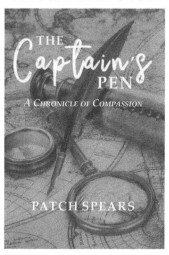

AVAILABLE ON AMAZON/BARNES AND NOBLE ETC
VISIT/CONTACT: patchspears.com OR @patchspears FB

Lightning Source UK Ltd.
Milton Keynes UK
UKHW022031281022
411289UK00003B/139